Healing Hurts
that Sabotage the Soul

Other books by Jan Johnson:
When Food Is Your Best Friend
Surrendering Hunger
Habakkuk: Staying Sane in a Crazy World

HEALING HURTS
that Sabotage the Soul

Curt Grayson & Jan Johnson

VICTOR BOOKS

A DIVISION OF SCRIPTURE PRESS PUBLICATIONS INC.
USA CANADA ENGLAND

This book includes some material that has been adapted and incorporated from *Creating a Safe Place* by Curt Grayson and Jan Johnson.

The Twelve Steps are reprinted and adapted with permission of Alcoholics Anonymous World Services, Inc. Permission to reprint and adapt The Twelve Steps does not mean that AA has reviewed or approved the content of this publication, nor that AA agrees with the views expressed herein. AA is a program of recovery from alcoholism. Use of The Twelve Steps in connection with programs and activities which are patterned after AA, but which address other problems, does not imply otherwise.

Scripture quotations are from the *Holy Bible, New International Version®*. Copyright © 1973, 1978, 1984 by International Bible Society. Used by permission of Zondervan Publishing House. All rights reserved.

Editor: Pamela T. Campbell
Cover Design: Scott Rattray
Cover Photo: Aaron Jones Studios
Interior Illustrations: Karl Edwards

Library of Congress Cataloging-in-Publication Data

Grayson, Curt.
  Healing hurts that sabotage the soul/by Curt Grayson, Jan Johnson.
    p. cm.
  ISBN 1-56476-449-4 (pbk.)
    1. Christian life. 2. Spiritual healing. I. Johnson, Jan, 1952– . II. Title.
  BV4501.2.G734 1995
  248.4–dc20   95-2861
                                                                                    CIP

1   2   3   4   5   6   7   8   9   10   Printing / Year   99   98   97   96   95

VICTOR BOOKS
A Division of SP Publications, Inc.
1825 College Avenue
Wheaton, Illinois 60187

To the New Hope Support Group
at First Evangelical Free Church, Fullerton, California
and Free to Choose, Hope Chapel,
Hermosa Beach, California

WE WOULD LIKE TO THANK:

Earl, whose words and silence helped create a safe place,
and my family, who, even through the stormy times,
let me know that I was still loved.

—Curt

My husband Greg and my children Jeff and Janae
who have walked through this process
of self-examination with me,
and who encouraged me while I walked,
talked, and dreamt this book.

—Jan

CONTENTS

PART I
Moments of Truth

CHAPTER ONE

Revealing Who We Are

What do you say to Christians who:

- study the Bible and pray regularly, but still fight bouts of sadness they can't explain?
- feel distant or resentful toward God when things go wrong?
- feel guilty because even though they have "the answer" in Christ, that answer doesn't seem to work for them?

These empty valleys of the Christian life can become dark nights of the soul where we wonder if God can still see us. Many times, however, God breaks the depths of these valleys into wide open spaces in which we can discover that knowing Christ amounts to a great deal more than attending worship services, getting together with friends from church, reading a devotional book, or listening to Christian radio. These moments of truth force us to reveal parts of ourselves no one has ever seen. We show them to Christ, fearing He may not be pleased, but instead He takes our hand and walks with us through a time of examining ourselves in light of God's grace and mercy.

We offer you ourselves in this book. We did more than research this material—Curt as a marriage and family therapist; Jan as a journalist and Bible teacher—we lived it as we've both led groups in which others also found safe places for themselves. We offer you now our stories as partners on the journey.

Curt's Journey

I was about to enter graduate school to fulfill what I thought was God's will for my life to become a family counselor. One night, while talking to a friend, I felt my heart begin to pound. My mind raced as if I were on some kind of drug that slammed me into hyperspace. My body felt squashed, my face got tight, and my hands shook. I tried to walk outside because I was sweating so much. I thought I was either dying or going crazy. Was this an out-of-body experience? Would it ever end?

That time it did end. But it kept coming back. I struggled to understand what was happening to me. I was trying to live a good life. I went to church, sang in the choir, read my Bible, and prayed regularly.

After the doctor screened for other physical causes for these symptoms, he concluded I was probably having panic attacks. I was afraid to tell Christian people about them because I thought they would think I had mental problems. Then I tried to spiritualize them away. I figured I had some terrible sin in my life, so I asked for forgiveness. I listened to Christian radio programs all the time so I could become more spiritual. I followed people's advice to "claim the victory," but the victory eluded me every time.

I felt completely alone. It seemed that no one, including God, could reach inside me and calm the craziness there. I had no answers—only questions—and I was giving up hope that I could regain control. I went through three years of soul searching—tears, fear, prayer, suicidal thoughts, failed relationships, and advice from well-meaning friends.

I ended up going to a perceptive Christian counselor who asked me about my childhood. The more we talked, the more I saw that my panic attacks were due to re-pressed pain from growing up in an alcoholic family. I knew that my parents had struggled with alcohol, but I thought I had put behind me the things of the past and been spared that pain. In fact, I thought that because of my difficulties growing up, I was tougher and more skilled in dealing with anything or anyone in life. I thought, *I can't be having panic attacks. They happen to other people, not to me.*

As I went to counseling and support groups, I learned how vulnerable and human I really was. I realized, much to my relief, that I was not alone. There were others like me who had gone through similar experiences even though they didn't grow up in an alcoholic family. I talked about my feelings of growing up, feeling responsi-ble for taking care of my mom emotionally, and how that affects me even today. I felt relieved when I discovered the attacks didn't mean I was crazy. They represented old patterns that needed attention and re-adjustment.

During my attacks, I began to reach out to others instead of isolating myself. Sometimes I called other peo-ple on the telephone and talked as best I could. As pain-ful as the attacks were, I eventually began to sense that God loves me. He was allowing the pain to rise to the surface and dissipate. I trusted that He knew what I was ready to remember.

Even after several years, these attacks still occur at times. I see them as warnings that I feel isolated and that I need to talk about a problem. They show me that I'm once again trying to be too many things to too many people.

Jan's Journey

Imagine for a moment a whiz-kid pastor's wife who teaches Bible studies, sponsors teens, sings a mean alto in the church choir, and gives down-to-earth advice. That was me. A women's ministry leader once told me, "You have so much going for you—you must intimidate the wives of the other pastors on staff."

Imagine also a wife and mother who is demanding and impatient, who can't stand herself. That was also me. I knew these two people existed, but I had no idea what to do about either of them. I didn't like being two people, but nothing seemed to help. I felt so hopeless that I sometimes pondered ways to end my life. I desperately wanted to be the same person all the time, but I struggled to know why I couldn't.

What confused me most was that I had such great intentions. I loved God and I loved serving Him, but I couldn't stand people for very long. I wanted to be kind and loving, but it seemed as if a terrible boogeyman haunted me and forced me to be someone I didn't want to be. I didn't know how to solve problems or work through feelings. I only knew how to cry and yell.

This dilemma simmered on the back burner until my husband told me that he hated me and planned to leave me. That hot Sunday afternoon he produced a list of 10 criticisms I'd fired at him before work one morning. As I listened to him talk, I knew he was right. I also knew that asking forgiveness would not be enough this time. I had to change.

I began eating constantly to numb the pain. Food has always been my best friend anyway, but now it was my only friend. I finally attended an eating disorders support group at a church several miles away and there found a group of Christians who weren't afraid to admit how far short of the glory of God they'd fallen and how much pain they felt because of it. At first, I hated their honesty! Later, I grew to love it. They understood what it meant to be two people you didn't like. The group understood that like them, I ate because I was angry or feeling sorry for myself.

Down the hall from my support group was another group for adult children of "dysfunctional families," whatever that meant. I tiptoed into their meeting one night and found that what they said about themselves described me too. I created chaos wherever I went. I tried to control everything around me to protect myself, to avoid ever being hurt by anybody. I had never recognized these tendencies in myself before, but after hearing group members share, I knew these tendencies were true for me as well.

By seeing myself in others, I was able to admit my faults. I discovered that I had desperately wanted to please others (which explained the whiz-kid persona), but inside I was raging from hurts I didn't even know I had (which explained the demanding, impatient crazed persona). When I saw these fellow strugglers accept, and even laugh about our common faults, I felt a growing assurance that God loved me even with my faults.

So I turned to God, speaking out more boldly than before. I spent days and nights screaming out those vengeful Psalms I found buried in the Bible. Many times I sat on gravestones in the cemetery across the street from my house and wept. Even though I was rapidly changing, my marriage wasn't. My husband had moved from hate to indifference. That's when I faced God on a gravestone one day, saying, "Even if he leaves me, I am grateful for what I am learning from You."

After a while, my husband began attending a support group as well. There he emptied himself of his frustration and anger—feelings pastors aren't supposed to have, right? It has taken years for our marriage to heal, which further schooled me in God-given tools of working through my anger and sadness. Now, I see that my brokenness is my greatest asset because it forces me to turn to God and live in His grace. This journey has given me a small taste of union with God, and it has whet my appetite to the point that I am more hungry for God than I've ever been before.

This book is about living the examined Christian life and the chaotic moments which lead us down paths of self-examination. We've described the chaotic moments as *we* experienced them. Perhaps you're experiencing your own chaotic moments. Nothing that worked for you before works now. A distant, troubled voice inside you wonders if God has deserted you.

When we go through these struggles, the best path is to look at patterns from the past, often established in childhood, that have set us up to protect ourselves. Without realizing it, we may have developed masks to keep ourselves from being hurt. These masks can block the vulnerability required to surrender ourselves to God and to connect with other people.

Our goals in writing this book are to come along side you who are struggling, to tell you some stories to help you see yourself, and to walk with you through a process of self-examination. Our goals are not to send you into a cycle of endless Christian self-improvement or to urge you to bash your upbringing. We want to tell the Good News that God is there, not only for the dynamic Christian, but also for the hurt and the frustrated: "A bruised reed He will not break, and a smoldering wick He will not snuff out, till He leads justice to victory" (Matt. 12:20). We want to play a part in removing barriers between you and the people around you so you can glimpse the healing that is available in the Kingdom of God. We want to clear the path between you and God so you can relate to Him in a more authentic way.

We have revealed part of our personal journeys here and will continue to tell you about ourselves and others because we believe that true stories are a powerful tool for change. We have changed names and camouflaged details at times because we wish to allow enough privacy to tell the truth, cutting as close to the bone as possible. We also want to maintain the anonymity of those whose lives have helped make up the fabric of this book.

Both of us were surprised to find how much our self-protective ways of thinking, feeling, and behaving were rooted in the way we responded to growing up. Even though families do their best to stay away from the denial, blame, isolation, and anger of our culture, nearly every family is tainted by them. So while we do talk about tendencies in families, we don't blame our parents. All parents carry an incredible load and nobody does the job as well as they would like.

Parts I and II of this book set you on the path of self-examination with stories and insights about patterns people develop from childhood and keep using as adults. As you read about how children develop masks, you might get a glimpse of pain and anger you have buried. You may also recognize flaws in yourself that you don't like. Often these realizations are not easy to process, and you may be tempted to give up because it's such a soul-searching experience. But the confusion and questioning are with the journey as you learn how to become vulnerable to God and find freedom from the self-protection of the past.

Part III describes the tools needed to examine yourself in light of the information already offered. We'll ask you to be willing to hear your deepest cries, but we'll also ask you to seek God in finding a friend or group with whom you can discuss these ideas. Finally, in Part IV, we'll present tools for building a resilient faith to help you bounce back from difficulties and feel equipped with God's reassuring love.

Each chapter closes with questions that many people ask about this journey. We hope that if you have questions, these might be yours. We've also included questions for your personal reflection in helping you to work through the chapter's content in your life. These questions are also ideal for group study and so we urge you to discuss these questions with a partner or group.

A special note to anyone who has quit attending church: We were both on the verge of joining those ranks when we began this process. We were burned out Christians, tired church leaders who believed the church was no longer helping us get our spiritual needs met. We had misunderstood God and were worn out from trying to understand Him. We pray that if you feel this way, you will allow God to re-ignite your faith in Him and help you find safe places to heal your hurts.

CHAPTER TWO

Three Pilgrims' Progress

As God's flashlight moves around the rooms of our lives and we begin to examine the obscure corners and deep closets, we find fellow travelers who are willing to walk with us. What a relief to find other people who, although they outwardly appear to be content and self-sufficient, are actually struggling but unrelenting in their quest to develop a more authentic relationship with God. As they share their stories and their burdens, their experiences become part of God's flashlight, shedding insights so that we can see our own healing paths more clearly. Here are stories from three pilgrims on this journey.

Susanna's Journey

As my friend and I sat on her bed and she talked in the dimming twilight about the love, joy, and peace that accepting Christ would bring, I knew I wanted it. On top of that, I would receive eternal life.

How could she know—she couldn't—that I had planned to commit suicide the night before? If I had gone through with it, she and everybody else would have wondered how a "Most Likely to Succeed" award recipient and homecoming queen nominee could take her own life?

As she talked about how we don't deserve God's love, I agreed. We prayed together, and I accepted Christ. Then I fell on her bed and cried for a long time.

A few months later, I fell on my own bed and cried. All my old feelings of chaos and anger resurfaced. I felt empty and alone again. *Was I really saved?* I wondered. *Maybe I should go forward at the youth meeting again.* I did, but it didn't rekindle those early feelings of joy and peace. That could mean only one thing—I had disappointed God or angered Him. Maybe I wasn't good enough to be His child.

But, from my experiences at home, I knew how to make people love me. I would make God love me. I would be good, work hard, and help anyone I could.

Taking care of people had always filled my emptiness. When my mother divorced my father and threw him out of the house, I visited him every day at his apartment where I would find him drunk. Many times he didn't have food, so I sneaked food out of our house to him.

Later, when I became a missionary, I thought, *Wouldn't God be pleased with my sacrifice? How could He not love me for this?* Working in an orphanage in Kenya filled the emptiness, but whenever I saw a lonely and hurting child, I would see myself as a child and start to cry. My well-meaning Christian friends urged me, "Pray harder, read the Bible more, and trust God to meet all your needs." I did these things, but I felt worse. I was afraid to tell my friends that their solutions weren't working—they might think I wasn't spiritual.

I decided the answer was to work in a more difficult country, so I signed up to go to a Hindu nation where anyone who was caught trying to convert someone received a seven-year prison sentence. Being a martyr had a double appeal for me: I could make God proud of me, and I could also die, which would relieve the emotional pain that kept coming back.

After three years, an illness forced me stateside. I became so depressed that I found myself in the office of a Christian counselor.

"What was your home life like?" he asked me.

"My father is an alcoholic, but that's been an advantage," I explained. "I'm stronger and more compassionate because of my background. Unlike other people, I adapt easily because I never knew what was going to happen when I was growing up."

The counselor smiled at me and quietly explained how a family with an alcoholic is likely to magnify our culture's tendency toward denial, blame, anger, and isolation. He said my depression was rooted in these tendencies.

I stared at him. It sounded as if he were speaking a foreign language—I couldn't believe it. He gave me an address of a support group meeting at a nearby church and suggested I try it out.

The meeting shocked me. People who looked so together and knew so much Scripture felt as discouraged as I did. As they shared their stories, I cried. Even when I didn't stop crying, no one acted as if I were wrong or silly. Several people talked to me afterward.

I went to more meetings, crying through the first six. I found I didn't have to pretend to be a "SuperChristian" anymore. I could be exactly who I was and still be loved. It felt like a family.

At the seventh meeting, I admitted that I had used the mission field as an escape because I didn't know how to handle life. I went to "save the world"—just as I'd been saving my father, or so I thought. I expected the people in the group to be horrified, but they smiled and nodded. They understood me. Through *their* understanding and acceptance, I began to sense *God's* acceptance of me. I began telling God how I really felt. I didn't have to perform to get Him to love me.

After a while, it was tempting to pretend to be wonderful again. Now, I see that this is a lifelong process of connecting with God and believing He loves me as I am. With each transition in life, I seem to have to review where I've been and remind myself of the truths that God loves me and works in me.

Matt's Journey

"It's because you pretend to be OK," my sister Marcia challenged me. "I see the painful look in your eyes. Your voice quivers. You're nervous."

I didn't know what to say to my sister. We had just finished a serious talk about how I was more than normally afraid to ask girls out.

She quieted her voice and said, "Matt, I see this fear in you because I'm the same way. We don't have to do this. We don't have to live to please people."

I didn't like what she was saying, and it showed.

"Trust me," she said gently. "I've caused major problems in my marriage because I don't speak up for myself. Believe it or not, it works better when I express what I think and feel. Then my husband understands me and we work through things. You hide what you're thinking and feeling too."

I knew Marcia thought my problem with women had deeper roots, but I wasn't sure. My career was also a problem. I had worked with several Christian advertising companies, but I never stuck with anything. I drifted from job to job. I lacked confidence and I had no goals.

I was afraid to get close to people. I didn't initiate friendships easily. My upbringing taught me that if you get close to people, they go away or send you away.

I remember being six years old and feeling confused about why I couldn't live at home anymore. Because my parents were missionaries in Pakistan, I went away to boarding school. Several times we elementary boys got the tar kicked out of us by high school boys in the same dorm. Since then, I've been afraid of people who were older than me or who had authority over me.

Returning to boarding school the second time was even worse. After living with my family on furlough for a year, a boarding school teacher mistook my sadness for laziness and sent me to the principal's office many times. I often wrote punishment sentences 500 times. At the end of the year, she recommended that I repeat that grade, and my parents decided to trust her judgment. This validated my suspicion that I was not a smart person.

The next year my grades improved dramatically, but the other boys called me "Dummy." One boy, who had also done poorly but was not held back, would say, "You can't talk to me because you're dumb," whenever I beat him in tether ball. Throughout school, I was a year behind my original class and I never forgot it.

Vacations were strained too. When my parents wanted me to get up and read a Bible verse in our supporting churches, fear gripped me. As I grew older, I learned to get through life by playing roles. It was like entertaining people. I could keep people at a distance by acting as if I were someone else.

My mother wanted to be perceived as a responsible missionary who did her job efficiently and correctly. She kept the house fastidiously clean. I'm sure *she* didn't feel this way, but *I* always felt that all the small things she worried about were more important than her children's feelings. She fussed at us about being late because it made a bad impression. I felt tense whenever our family went somewhere together.

As the years passed, I learn to distance myself from my parents. It was so painful to be with them and then leave them every year in the fall to go back to boarding school, that I made sure I *never* got close to them. When I came back to the States for college, I continued to keep people at a distance. Small group interaction threatened me. I didn't go to Bible studies unless I knew everyone well and trusted them.

When my parents announced that they planned to return to the States for good, Marcia urged me to prepare myself. I tried counseling and a support group, but I felt uncomfortable. At one of the groups, though, I told Gil, one of the guys, how his story reminded me of myself. We ended up standing in the parking lot for hours as I told him my experiences. I had never been so honest. I was afraid to talk at the meetings, so I came late and stayed late to talk to Gil. His experiences were different from mine, but he had that same feeling that nobody really wanted to be his friend.

When things happened during the week that devastated me, I worked through them as best I could and then Gil and I talked about them after the meeting. Sometimes we went out to eat. During dinner, Gil would stop eating and ask me: "How did you feel? Did you want to ignore that woman? What exactly do you think upset your boss?" His questions helped me stop living in a fog. I tried to figure out what I was feeling and why. When he struggled, he would make himself accountable to me, saying, "I'm going to work hard on not trying to impress my boss, OK?" The next week, I'd ask him how it went.

When my parents arrived, they were concerned that I wasn't married yet, and that I hadn't figured out what I was going to do with my life.

"You need a family. You need a career. What's wrong?" they asked me.

Marcia tried to explain what we were both going through. I sat a few feet away, feeling protective of my parents and wanting Marcia to be quiet, but I knew that what she was saying was true.

My mother kept saying, "Don't talk to me about this." My father warned us against listening to psychologists. I tried to explain that this had to do with my spiritual life too, but it was difficult for them to listen. Finally, my mom talked about her feelings of abandonment because her mother left her with an aunt when she was only six years old. I saw that my parents had hurts of their own, and maybe they covered them up with workaholism.

I called Gil when I got home and we went for a walk. I admitted that as a kid in boarding school I felt abandoned by God. I tried so hard not to cry, but it all came out. That has helped me more than anything else to work through my feelings of abandonment and insecurity. I don't beat myself up all the time now. I am more accepting of others because I've heard how other people struggle. I don't feel trapped in depression because I know I am accepted even when I'm angry or upset.

Donna's Journey

"What was your home life like?" my boss asked me.

I was annoyed. All I had done was ask his advice about a problem with my teenage son, and now he, a minister, insinuated that I came from a problem family.

"Why do you ask?" I replied, keeping my usual calm church-secretary manner in tact.

"Because so many feelings you describe fit the book I've been reading about how people who grow up in alcoholic families respond to life."

"That's silly," I said, dismissing him with a polite smile. "My parents were not drunks. That's for sure." I began seething. I knew what he was talking about because I'd typed up some material for him.

As the day wore on, I began to remember my dad talking about how Grandpa used to drink. Later, by the copy machine, I quizzed my pastor/boss/friend: "Would it affect me if my grandfather drank a lot?" He said that it could, depending on how my father reacted to his up-bringing. *Oh great,* I thought, *now we were getting knee-deep into psychology!*

When I asked what he meant, he said that if my dad imitated his father's erratic attitudes (even though he didn't drink), I could have picked up those tendencies from him.

I sat at my desk and pulled out the material I had typed. I thought about my problems with my son. I saw that if I were honest, the material described me: seeking approval, judging myself without mercy, struggling with intimate relationships. This wasn't, however, the "me" that my church friends knew. They knew me as an efficient good-deed-doer who whizzed through projects, never made typing errors, and always stayed late to finish her work. They never guessed that I was still so keyed up when I got home that anything my husband or son said set me off. I would take my husband's simple question, "Are there any clean shirts?" as an attack. Many times he did the laundry to keep from stirring me up.

But I was never pacified. I constantly got angry with my husband and son and I felt discouraged about it. It seemed that no matter how hard I tried, happiness and contentment were only temporary. I would never be that terribly nice Christian I wanted to be.

That day in the office I began to wonder if my dad felt the way I did. He had been an only child, abandoned in infancy by his mother. He was raised by a stern grandmother and his alcoholic father.

Dad could be warm, kind, and caring much of the time, but he was quick to explode. He could be talking gently to me, handing me a glass of iced tea, when Mom might ask, "Why didn't you fix me a glass of tea?" Then he would start yelling. I was scared and unsure of what would happen next with him.

Mom was also an only child. She grew up in a loving, but strict, legalistic home. She had to toe the line at all times and she treated my brother and me the same way. I learned early that if I talked back, I would get slapped or have my mouth washed out with soap. I learned that it was not OK to express real feelings—only what was acceptable to others.

As an adult, I unloaded this anger at my husband and son. I acted just like my father—swearing, slamming doors, spitting out sarcastic put-downs. It was so ironic. I had promised God I would never treat my son the way my parents treated me, but I did it anyway. I disciplined my son unfairly and made unreasonable demands on him—that was the only way I knew how to be a parent.

After that day at work, I read the books my boss recommended and I even went to a support group. After the first meeting, I told my husband, "These people are a bunch of whiners," but by the next Tuesday I wanted to go back. I saw that they weren't whiners, just more open than most people at church. That honesty and acceptance drew me until I became one of them, sharing my true self.

After several years of looking at myself, I've discovered more appropriate ways to express my anger. I've learned not to be so controlling of people. The other day, my now 22-year-old son asked my advice for the first time because he knows that now he'll get a simple opinion instead of a lecture.

My temperament has changed completely. I rarely seethe with anger. I can respond to people around me based on what they're saying to me rather than reacting out of my feelings.

I left my position as church secretary because my husband and I agreed that I needed time to get to know myself. Now that I've shed my "Outstanding Christian" role, I enjoy going to church and I'm working again as a church secretary. It's different this time. I'm more calm because I don't have to be perfect. I do the best I can, but on some days I don't get everything done.

I'm experimenting with being honest. The other day, my mom was complaining about Dad's angry outburst. "Have you ever told Dad how you feel about his behavior?" I asked.

"No. He wouldn't like that," she said, surprised.

I pushed on. "If you start telling him when he makes you feel uncomfortable, he might stop. Tell him you're not going to put up with that anymore."

My mother stared.

"I know this, Mom, because I have acted the same way. We both act like Grandpa when we're upset and it's not appropriate."

My mom seemed offended and she didn't respond, yet she has brought it up now and then over the last year. I've left the door open.

I also talked to Dad that day. I was surprised that he was so vulnerable. He started talking about his childhood. I listened and asked questions. We talked so long we missed our dinner reservations. I have compassion for my mom and dad now. They did the best they could with what they knew.

This search for emotional wholeness turned out to be more than that. It became a discovery of God and His love for me.

Hearing other people's stories gives us hope that we're not crazy or unspiritual. Even missionaries and church personnel struggle with a shadow side — no one is exempt. As we listen to fellow pilgrims tell about their inner selves, it is easier for us to let our deeper thoughts and feelings come forth — those things that have made us feel less than whole, less than Christian, and less than human. We begin to trust that God knows these secret thoughts and feelings and that He wants to work in us to make us whole and free, to help us connect with others in a genuine way, and to convince us that we're loved by Him.

Personal Reflection

Perhaps these stories have brought some questions to mind about your own life. Take a minute to quiet yourself. Ask God to reveal anything you need to know or acknowledge about yourself. Then answer the following questions as honestly as possible.

● With whom do you identify most — Susanna, Matt, or Donna? With what exactly did you relate?

● If you could have changed one thing in the family in which you grew up, what would it be? Why?

● What would you most like to tell your parents today, but perhaps do not feel the freedom to say?

● If your parents could change one circumstance about your childhood years, what do you think they would choose to change?

● In what ways did God watch out for you as a child?

● What topics did your family avoid talking about?

● Who in your house did you trust most?

● What feelings was your family uncomfortable with?

● If you have a friend with whom you could share these answers, whom would that be?

CHAPTER THREE

Questions at the Crossroads

What must I do to feel loved?
What must I do to feel valued?

We believe these are the core questions of life. Many people come face to face with themselves only a few times in life where they ask themselves these questions.

Usually those moments occur when people see that the answers they've chosen thus far aren't sufficient. *I will get married, and then I will be loved,* they think. Only the marriage doesn't provide the deep abiding love they need, or perhaps the marriage doesn't even last. Or the career that once gave them such value feels empty, or the children who gave them meaning have moved away.

When these questions—*What must I do to feel loved? What must I do to feel valued?*—are not answered, we find ourselves searching. We may struggle to be close to people, but we can't. We may want to make circumstances work in our favor, but we can't. We may want help from God, but we can't seem to get it. We may even feel as if other Christians know some secret formula that we don't know.

Some people let these questions eat away at them for years like a nagging itch until they're ready to begin a journey of self-examination such as the one we describe in this book. For others, a painful crisis erupts. If they recognize this crisis as a time of waking up to these questions, they take a deeper look at themselves. If not, they may blame others for the crisis and never look at their motives and patterns.

Awakenings

For many people, it's as if the buried pain and frustration of their past have slowly filled up a holding tank. All at once, that tank explodes, perhaps in one of the following ways.

Divorce

Some spouses are surprised by their own divorce. "I knew the marriage needed help," they say, "but why does my spouse suddenly want out? When did the relationship deteriorate this much? Why was my spouse content one day and at the end of the rope the next? What is it I didn't see?"

Meanwhile, the spouse tells the pastor: "She [or he] is a different person at home. I love her, but I can't stand living with her. I've put up with her moodiness for years and now I'm through."

Other times, a spouse will leave home saying: "I'm tired of being married to someone I don't know. Sometimes he pulls away from me; other times, he's defensive. I could say, 'Is it OK if I strangle you?' and he would say, 'Whatever you want.' I refuse to be ignored for the rest of my life. I've had it. Don't try to fix this—I don't want it fixed. I just want to be free."

Compulsive behaviors

When we don't feel good about ourselves, anything— even a good thing—becomes addiction-like when used to prop up our flagging self-esteem. What begins as an innocent desire to look decent in a swimming suit turns into an eating disorder. Having a few beers becomes the only possible way to relax. Some people may find themselves overspending, reading pornography, or stealing knickknacks from stores whenever they feel sad or bored or need a reward.

Four-thirty P.M. was the best part of Rick's day. After answering newspaper ads, he could finally plant himself in front of the TV to watch those east coast basketball games. On particularly depressing days, he went with a friend to a pizza place to watch the games on the big screen.

Then the TV watching became a constant escape. He began watching movies late into the night and then sleeping into the next day. He spent the money he did make occasionally on books and videos instead of helping out the family. The chair in front of the TV was the only place he wanted to be and he stayed there. He knew he was using TV to escape, but he had no idea what to do about it. He wasn't surprised when his wife Linda confronted him: "Sometimes I wonder if you're really looking for a job. It seems like all you ever do is watch TV."

"I can't pay the bills," Rick told her. "I can't find a job. When I do get one, it's wrong. I watch TV to help me forget it all."

"But you forget me and the kids and your responsibilities, even your health," Linda challenged. "You won't even go to the doctor."

"It's an escape," Rick explained. "I know you're going to ask how the job hunt went. I know I'll have nothing to report and my answer will sound shallow. I feel so bad that I can hardly face you. It's easier to look at the TV."

Rick's problem got worse before it got better. It took him a long time to see that his dependency on TV and reading was a signal that something inside was awry. Because of the job search he was in great pain, but he was also masking feelings of never being good enough. Voices from his past were coming back to haunt him — *You don't try! You're lazy! You always get into trouble!*

He had been told these things as a college student and had never faced whether or not they were true.

Failure on the job

Sometimes when people lose a promotion or even their job, it's because their past feelings begin leaking into their work life. Maybe they don't show up as they should. Or they outshine others in achieving goals, but are unable to manage their tempers, especially with key personnel. When they're fired, they tell us that they don't know how that business or their bosses will ever get along without them. Or perhaps they sigh in relief that they failed because success was wearing them down physically and emotionally.

Illness

Some medical doctors now give their patients question-naires about family background because so much of illness (perhaps 80%) is stress related.[1] Stress heightens the body's susceptibility to allergies, asthma, skin rashes, arthritis, cancer, infections, jaw disorders, immune system diseases, and collagen diseases such as Lupus. Problems such as headaches, constipation, diarrhea, muscle tension, and sleep disorders may be warnings that something is wrong.

Doctors now recommend support groups and therapy when they suspect the patient's illness is rooted in past stresses. For example, in the treatment of anorexia doctors recommend support groups and therapy for the entire family because medical treatment alone does not help.

Posttraumatic Stress Disorder (PTSD)

PTSD is most often associated with Vietnam War veterans who have recurring flashbacks of gruesome battlefield experiences. They remember vividly the sights, sounds, and smells of battle, not only as they dream, but also while they are awake. Some adults experience PTSD as they recall traumatic childhood events that they repressed long ago. They tried to forget the "wars" of their childhood, but the pain remained.

Panic attacks

Panic attacks are a physical response to pain that can no longer be repressed. All at once, a person experiences heart palpitations, shortness of breath, dizziness, sweating, or vomiting. Thoughts fly through the person's head faster than he or she can handle them. For example, agoraphobics (people who fear being in places or situations from which escape would be physically or psychologically difficult) often experience panic attacks in open spaces, especially crowded ones. When sufferers experience situations similar to ones buried in their past, their bodies replay the pain and helplessness in this outward form.

The Nagging Itch

The holding tank of buried pain and frustration does not explode for some people, but slowly leaks to the point that they find they're walking on soil that won't hold them from day to day.

Low-grade depression

Depressives feel unsettled with life, as if the thrill is gone. They're not as interested in people or projects, and so their jobs and close relationships usually have some rough edges. In addition, their relationship with God in prayer and Bible study doesn't seem to help them anymore.

Deep sadness

Deep sadness often occurs in adults who as children became extremely angry for some reason. That anger seethes within them and there seems to be no resolution to it. Sometimes they turn this anger inward and become deeply depressed. This "frozen rage" is buried deep within and can be difficult to recognize and treat.

Unexplainable fights with family members

People who have gotten along fine with their parents, children, or siblings now feel these family members are ignoring them or demanding too much of them. Leaving a towel on the bathroom floor or not cleaning up messes begin to bother these men and women like never before. Instead of saying nothing, they can't help but say something. Family members may feel they can't do anything that is pleasing or acceptable.

Inability to follow through

Nothing gets finished. Deadlines are missed, promises are broken, and ethics that once mattered are violated. The conscience catches up with this man or woman and says, *Is this the kind of person I want to be?* They don't like the way they're behaving, but they can't find the energy or courage to change.

Feeling as if they're faking life

The listlessness gets annoying as people attend meetings and activities they hate and compliment people for qualities they don't even respect. Thoughts and actions seem to be cover-ups for true desires. It becomes apparent they're not doing what they want to do.

Swallowed Up in Crisis

We do amazingly well at ignoring this restlessness and even dismissing crises, but if we're given enough time to think, it catches up with us. Vacations with unstructured time can be unpleasant. When friends or relatives come to visit, we may take stock of ourselves in relation to them and not like what we see. Job lay-offs bring back past feelings of loneliness and worthlessness. We find ourselves feeling like the same kid who used to lie in bed and stare at the ceiling, wondering, *What will become of me?*

These emotional upheavals are sometimes triggered by transitions between life stages, which come around every ten to fifteen years for most people in western culture. At these forks in the road, we reevaluate our life choices and ponder whether they turned out as we thought they would. We ask, *What do I really give to (and get from) my spouse, children, church, friends, work, community—and self? How do I live up to my commitments (career, marriage, kids), but make the changes I need to make?* If those questions become disturbing, we're likely to go on to face those core questions, as well: *What must I do to feel loved? What must I do to feel valued?*

Life transitions create a setting for intense soul-searching which occurs in three stages:

- leaving old values behind
- choosing new values
- trying to make those new values work

If we don't have the communication skills or self-confidence to make the changes we think we need to make, we can fall into despair. This is what Matt did when he kept changing jobs (Chapter 2). It gets even worse if we find ourselves in an intolerable situation (demeaning job, abusive marriage) and have no idea where we'll find the energy and courage to change it.

Sometimes people respond by changing nearly everything. They switch careers, leave a spouse, build a wall between their children and themselves, quit groups they've been a part of for years, stop or start going to church. They look for a new niche in life by developing new skills, establishing a different home base, and becoming an important member of a group they value. Yet they become frustrated if they don't advance within the new choices they've made, thinking, *What's wrong with me? Why can't I do the things others do? Do I have the courage to break out of my job or social group and try another?*

Adult life stages have been described well by adult development specialist Dr. Daniel Levinson.[2] Adults make their first choices about occupation, marriage, friendships, values, and dreams in their twenties. These choices may resemble their family's choices. For example: If the family was Christian, they're Christians. If Mom or Dad chose a particular profession such as a doctor or plumber, they might follow the same path. Or, they may decide their family's choices were poor and make opposite choices. *My parents were lazy, so I'll work hard. My parents didn't care about education, but I'm going to college.*

After this first choice, at least four transitions occur in which adults reevaluate their lives.

- *Changing the first choices (28-33)*
- *Mid-life transition (40-45)*
- *Middle adulthood transition (50-55)*
- *Late adult transition (60-65)*

Tyler faced his first struggle at the age 30 transition:

At 24, I finished graduate ministerial training. My heart had always been to serve God as the pastor of a church. I married a woman I met in college when we served together in a children's outreach ministry. She stole my heart from the first glance.

We moved to a new city together to start a church with hope and promise between us. We had three children right away and our church grew quickly. We moved from a storefront building to a huge facility in just a few years.

Then something weird started to happen. I was only thirty, but I felt as if I had no energy. It seemed as if no matter what great things happened at the church or how much my wife loved me, the great successes didn't matter. I was at a staff meeting one day and the youth minister who had never bothered me before got under my skin. He had always been kind of a smart mouth, but I couldn't take his digs anymore. I felt myself ready to explode, but I kept it in. I went home that night and it didn't get better. I walked up the driveway and slipped on one of my kid's skateboards and fell flat on my back. I got up and picked up my boy and for the first time, I slapped him across the face. The look of fear in his eyes is something I'll never forget. I was not normally a violent person and I couldn't believe I behaved that way. What was happening to me?

Many people think that the solution to their upheaval is to marry someone else, get a different job, or move to a different state. The problem is that we take ourselves (and our old baggage) with us. To truly face a crisis and wring all the good out of it we can, we need to reappraise the past and examine our long-held assumptions and traits. *How should I live my life—setting aside what my parents did or said and how I may have overreacted to it? How can I find an authentic relationship with God? What is it that God has put within my heart to do?* It's time to rethink past assumptions and seek truth.

As we do so, we stumble upon those core questions again: *What must I do to feel loved? What must I do to feel valued?* The answers to these questions are found within a relationship with God, but we each have to work out that relationship in such a way that the answers to those questions are real to us. That can happen as a crisis or as long years of slow disgust brings us to that prime moment of examining the patterns in our behavior and the motives driving them. We then bring this information about ourselves before God and cultivate the relationship at a deeper level. The crisis or nagging itch that functions as a detour from success becomes a path to developing a more honest faith and life.

We tend to put off the journey, ignoring the warning signs that all is not well with our soul. If we have the courage and support with God's help, we can move forward choosing to grow rather than exerting years of energy pretending we're fine. We begin by investigating the roots of our confusion and we see that this is not a new problem. It's as old as Adam and Eve.

You May Be Wondering . . .

Q *All this self-examination sounds so overwhelming. Should I wait?*

A Take it at your own pace. Don't isolate. Talk to others. Seek professional help, if necessary. Pray about this and ask God to show you what you need to know.

Q *What if I'm in one of those transitions and I'm ready to give up my occupation or my marriage?*

A If you're confused and emotionally charged, make as few changes as possible. Take the time for personal examination and then you'll know more about who you are, your choices, and God's will for your life.

Q *I have grown up in a Christian family, but I'm questioning what I've been taught about beliefs and behaviors. What's wrong with me?*

A This can happen at any age, but it occurs most often in the early twenties. This healthy separation from parents is part of normal development. It causes stress, however, because we may have thought we'd be like our parents. Working through this predicament involves letting God help us sort out what we believe and don't believe, and who we need to become, apart from our parents. Many times, we come around to embracing the positive values of our parents, but choose to change the behaviors and approaches to life that haven't worked well for us.

Q *What if I've begun to think about suicide?*
A If you have suicidal intentions or severe suicidal feelings, seek professional help immediately. Call a suicide hot line and find out about local counseling centers or outpatient county facilities. Stay in touch with people. Talk with someone you trust. Carry a telephone number for a suicide hotline with you.

It helps to remember that suicidal feelings are not uncommon, and they are different from suicidal intentions. Suicidal feelings are usually a strong desire to escape while suicidal intentions mean that the person may have the suicide planned in detail and does not intend to seek help.

If outpatient treatment doesn't help, don't be afraid to be hospitalized. After the crisis subsides, outpatient treatment and support groups will probably meet your needs.

Suicidal feelings often signal that the pain of our past is too great and we want to escape. The better choice, however, if we're ready, is to take the journey step by step because things *do* get better.

Personal Reflection

Answer the following questions as honestly as possible. Take a minute to quiet yourself before answering them, and ask God to reveal to you anything you need to know.

● Of the crises listed, which, if any, have you experienced: divorce, failure on the job, illness, posttraumatic stress disorder, panic attacks?

● Have you experienced any of these more subtle problems: low-grade depression, deep sadness, unexplainable fights with family members, inability to follow through, feeling as if you're faking life? If so, how do you act when you experience it?

● How have you reevaluated yourself in these transitions?

● What would you most like to have happen in your life regarding these choices: career, marriage, relationship with God?

● What are you doing to work out these choices?

PART II
Hurts that Sabotage the Soul

CHAPTER FOUR

The Handicap of Being Human

The inability to be the Christian we would like to be is not a newfangled psychological malady: Chronic Faithlessness Syndrome. It's a universal problem for humankind. It flourishes when we pretend it's not there and it blooms wherever it's planted. The garden is the entire human race, and the growing season began with the Fall of humanity.

Adam and Eve experienced the painful regret and dashed hopes many people feel today. What could have been more "downwardly mobile" than being banished from the Garden of Eden? What could have been more shaming to them as parents than for one of their children to murder another, as Cain killed Abel?

After the Fall, Adam and Eve found that thorns and thistles grew not only from the ground, but also between each other. Part of the curse was that they would try to control each other: "Your desire will be for your husband, and he will rule over you" (Gen. 3:16). We can only guess how worthless they may have felt as the curse produced turmoil in the key areas that supply self-worth: making a living (tilling the fields) and childbearing (Gen. 3:16-19). This first family in history splintered as its members reacted with denial, blame, isolation and acting out of anger. These four tendencies have been handed down through families for generations until they have permeated every home and every culture.

Denial
"they hid from the Lord God"

We tend to think that most of life's problems are like hiccups; they'll go away if we ignore them long enough. This can grow into denial—acting as if painful events never occurred, pretending to be fine when we're not. Adam and Eve's behavior illustrates three rules for denial,[1] which set them up for failure and disappointment.

Don't talk

After the couple disobeyed God by eating from the tree of knowledge of good and evil, they didn't seek God in repentance and despair. They didn't approach God as children who trust their parents do, saying, "Look what we've done. We're sorry. What can we do?" Instead, they hid (Gen. 3:8). When God confronted them, they didn't admit guilt or ask for forgiveness.

Don't trust

When the serpent said Adam and Eve wouldn't die if they ate from the tree of the knowledge of good and evil, he contradicted God's words (Gen. 3:4-5). Adam and Eve trusted the serpent instead of God, the one who had given them every reason to trust Him. He had provided their needs and talked with them in the garden. They didn't even ask God about this serpent's statement, as a trusting child would ask a parent, "Didn't you say . . .?"

Don't feel

Even though Adam and Eve may have felt great sorrow, none was recorded in the Bible passage. Nor was it recorded that they pleaded with God to let them stay in the garden. The only feeling mentioned is Adam's fear: "I heard You in the garden, and I was afraid because I was naked; so I hid" (Gen. 3:10). Even then, Adam sounds as if he were defending his behavior, not admitting fear.

Adam and Eve then busied themselves with a supposed solution—sewing together fig leaf garments which God eventually replaced (Gen. 3:7, 21). In the same way, we often busy ourselves with inadequate, temporary "solutions" when we're afraid to face feelings that overwhelm us. It's easier to buy a gift for someone we've hurt rather than apologize; it's easier to set up chairs for Bible study than to sit down and confess our sins to God.

Don't talk! Don't trust! Don't feel!

Denial appears to be a benign coping mechanism, but be aware that it has three faces: the good, the bad and the ugly.

The Good

Denial seems useful for children in helping them disregard painful experiences. Those who were abused physically or sexually may manage to block it from their memory. In reality, they store these experiences in the subconscious mind, which becomes a holding tank for pain. Perhaps God in His mercy allows this delay because children are not equipped to face this pain. It lays dormant until as mature adults, they can face it and work through it.

Even in the most ordinary circumstances, children are encouraged to deny feelings with comments such as, "Don't look so blue!" or "Chin up!" We may have even been molded into a "looking-good kid" who worked hard to earn those magic words — "You're looking good!" — from parents and coaches. If, as children, we learned to do whatever it took to look good in other people's eyes — pretending to be happy, hiding anger — as adults we continue this "looking-good kid" mask by hiding marital problems, financial struggles and broken dreams.

This kind of denial is mistakenly assumed to be good. Susanna (Chapter 2), for example, said she was better and stronger because of her childhood difficulties. Well-meaning Christians sanction denial by quoting Romans 8:28: "And we know that in all things God works for the good of those who love Him, who have been called according to His purpose." They imply that this verse means we should refuse to face the hurts of our past and how they're sabotaging our life in God. Instead, this verse encourages us to face reality because God can work in the midst of great pain to transform us into His likeness. Jan tells about how she was asked to understand this.

As a college student working in downtown New York City, my companions and I did a lot of street witnessing and participated in Bible studies in apartments. I was excited about sharing the love of Jesus in a place of such broken-heartedness.

After a month or so, a missionary came to visit our group and she pulled me aside.

"Jan, I sense that there are some hurts in your past, aren't there?"

"Well, yes," I replied. "I felt very depressed as a teenager, but that's all over now. I'm in Bible college."

"Maybe," she smiled. "My hope for you is that you could wear your hurts a little more easily. Put them out there on your sleeve. Let people know you're hurt and that God is with you in the middle of it. Don't pretend that God makes everything easy."

I was completely confused by what she said, but I said nothing.

After that, I noticed that I was quieter, that I listened more, that I seemed to connect better with people. As I look back, I see that this was the first of many clues I received that the best way to communicate God's love was not to minimize the pain of life, but to call on God's presence in the middle of it.

The Bad

Denial moves from good to bad when adults continue to block out painful experiences and store them in the holding tank of the subconscious mind. For example, Donna's husband (Chapter 2) told her over and over that her critical ways were killing him inside. She meant well, and she prayed about it for a day or two, but then another crisis occurred and she vented her anger by criticizing him.

The Ugly

When adults continue to ignore the truth about what they feel, the holding tank of the subconscious mind gets so full of hurt that it begins leaking in the form of crises and nagging itches. Facing the hurts is hard work and involves looking at patterns and roles developed in child-hood and carried into adulthood. It's not easy to admit these mistakes, find forgiveness, and develop new pat-terns. It doesn't feel good to do these things, but it's good for us. It provides a gateway to living before God and the world in a more authentic way.

Coming out of denial is difficult because we live in degrees of awareness. We see our destructive patterns clearly for a minute or two, and then we slip back into seeing ourselves as a "looking-good kid." Or a crisis passes, so we forget the problem and go on.

Blame
"It was her fault, God."

Adam blamed his sin on Eve. Eve blamed the serpent and the first blame loop formed (Gen. 3:12-13). They both tried to look good in God's eyes—as if people could manipulate God's opinion of them. The human tendency to shift responsibility away from ourselves is at work when we say:

- I wouldn't be this way except . . .
- If you hadn't said that to me, then . . .
- I can't help the way I am because . . .

Sometimes people reverse the flow of the blame and judge themselves without mercy. *Maybe it's my fault,* they think, even when logic disproves it. Blame becomes a way of life for many so that when a crisis occurs, they are much more concerned about who to blame than how to solve the crisis.

Isolation
"I was afraid because I was naked; so I hid."

When Adam and Eve heard God walking in the garden, they hid instead of walking with Him (Gen. 3:8-10). They isolated themselves from God rather than seeking comfort from God who was most able to give it.

It's as if humanity has condemned itself to solitary confinement. To keep up that "looking-good kid" mask, we can't let people know our less-than-perfect thoughts and feelings. This self-inflicted isolation makes us feel lonely.

Isolation is normal for those who grew up in homes in which parents did not express themselves openly and honestly. Open and genuine contact with others seems enticing, but also dangerous because as children they were told to keep feelings to themselves. As adults, reaching out to others is an awkward, even painful experience. They may feel that others hold back or reject them even when they don't. When they make acquaintance with people who express feelings easily, they may back away or even sabotage potentially open friendships by mistreating these people so they'll step away.

Acting Out of Anger
"So Cain was very angry, and his face was downcast."

When Cain's sacrifice wasn't as acceptable as that of his brother Abel, Cain became angry. God acknowledged Cain's normal feelings of anger, but urged him to "do what is right" (Gen. 4:6-7) by preparing another sacrifice. Instead, Cain killed his brother (Gen. 4:1-9), choosing to act on his anger.

Other people's successes can be threatening and even convince you that you'll never be good enough. If you dwell on these thoughts, you may become angry and let that anger erupt in inappropriate outbursts. If you explode, as Cain did, you may even lie to cover it up. When asked where Abel was, Cain lied to God: " 'I don't know,' he replied. 'Am I my brother's keeper?' " (Gen. 4:9)

If you are untrained in ways to express anger appropriately, you may instead:

- seethe so quietly that no one else suspects that you're angry.

- pick a fight in such a subtle way that you manipulate family, co-workers or friends into thinking they're angry
- dump anger immediately into the inner holding tank and force yourself to be nice.

The last is often called self-control, but it is denial. The anger has not been dismissed, only disguised.

Where We Learn These Reactions

We learned denial, blame, isolation and acting out anger from several sources. First, as we have seen, it seems to be part of the way humanity responds to life, a part of man's natural tendency to sin. No one taught Adam, Eve, or Cain to deny, blame, isolate, or act out anger. Since the Fall, we have inherited the handicap of the *sin nature* that needs to be retrained to follow a path of union with God.

As if that weren't enough, nearly every *culture*, promotes denial, blame, isolation, and angry reactions. Our culture, the second influence, pushes these reactions foward in these ways.

Denial

Seminars and books urge us to impress others with little regard of our inner selves. We're told to put our best foot forward even if the other is bruised and bleeding.

Blame

Our culture teaches us that no issue is settled until we have assessed blame. The true deviant in school yard squabbles (as if there were just one) must be found out and punished. When a plane crash occurs, the public is obsessed with knowing who was at fault. While the airline industry assesses blame in order to avoid more crashes, the public longs for a scapegoat.

Isolation

With society's increased mobility, many feel lonely and lack roots. We don't have a history with neighbors or fellow church members. Instead of relying on the people next door, we don't know them. Even people who have many friends and belong to several groups can discover they're not truly close to anyone.

Acting out anger in harsh and hateful ways

Our culture says that the way to feel better about having been cut off on the freeway is to cut off the offending driver, even if it means risking our lives and an expensive car. Working through anger with the time-proven methods of journaling, prayer, or talking with a friend are not what we see portrayed and glorified in the movies.

The third influence besides our human tendency to sin and our culture is the family in which we've grown up. This makes sense as we understand that the family is a microcosm of our culture and also a private enough setting to allow our tendency to sin to reveal itself fully. It may be difficult to accept the flaws in our parents' behavior, but they are normally flawed human beings who, even though they may have done the best they could, did not nurture us adequately. And if we become parents, we will not be adequately nurturing parents either. For example, even parents with the best intentions become distracted by illness or divorce and do not give children the love and attention they need. Or they may pass on cultural notions of God as a shaming and manipulating parent or as a distant, uninvolved parent. If we grew up in such a family, we now may have a skewed view of God and find it difficult to relate to Him. Since nearly every family needs more work in relationship skills, most of us lack some of the necessary skills to build loving, committed relationships with others.

David Seamands describes this chain reaction in his book *Healing for Damaged Emotions:*

Beginning with the first sin of Adam and Eve, there was set in motion a chain reaction of imperfect parenting, through failures and ignorance and mis-guided actions, and worst of all, through conditional love.[2]

This chain reaction may be part of the punishment of children for the sins of the fathers to the third and fourth generation (Deut. 5:9). Sin often hurts innocent bystand-ers, and in this instance, the sin of parents spills over to children and grandchildren. Yet this spillage of sin doesn't mean that we are doomed. Deuteronomy 5:10 adds that God shows "love to a thousand generations of those who love [Him] and keep [His] commandments." Loving God and allowing Him to transform us can make the difference.

Defeating the Heat of the Curse

The shadows of these three influences—culture, up-bringing, and the human tendency to sin—handicap our growth. Even though we love God, these influences may be bullying us around. The apostle Paul felt this keenly: "I know that nothing good lives in me, that is, in my sinful nature. For I have the desire to do what is good, but I cannot carry it out" (Rom. 7:18).

To unravel these influences, we can examine who we are and how we learned to be this way. We admit who we are, surrender that to God, and allow Him to form new patterns in us. This journey is a spiritual one at its core. It's a process of becoming a whole person who relates to God as the caring person that He is. It is sorting through layers of theology we've absorbed and examining the love of God we have not yet absorbed. It's coming to God and finding that only He can answer those core questions: *What must I do to feel loved? What must I do to feel valued?* It's understanding Him to say, "You don't have to do anything. I've done it all. Come to Me, and be with Me." The result of this process is that it frees us to obey Christ (John 8:32) as we shed the sinful "works of the flesh," and grow in the "fruit of the spirit" (see Gal. 5:22-23).

Many of us haven't thought about childhood for a long time. Perhaps we've blocked sad memories and reinforced good ones. Yet people are the sum of their experiences, and childhood feelings lie trapped within many of us, telling us what to do every day even though we don't realize it. The simplest way to do this is to examine how we developed in the family in which we grew up (Chapters 5–7) and the patterns we developed as adults (Chapters 8–10).

You May Be Wondering . . .

Q *Aren't you saying that we should blame our parents for our problems?*

A We don't examine the past for the purpose of shifting blame onto our parents; we do it to pinpoint our destructive patterns and find freedom from them. Still, some readers may feel defensive for their families, but given that all have sinned and fallen short of God's glory, what family is free of sinful tendencies? As people search their souls, the Spirit reveals what they need to know. It's important to be open to God to reveal the issues He wants disclosed.

Blaming parents is futile because most parents are well-meaning in their attempts to nurture children. Parents were affected by their own sin nature, culture, and upbringing. Many parents have made heroic attempts to filter out these influences and they have passed on much less of the denial, blame, isolation, and anger. As a result, our struggle is not as severe as it might have been.

Q *Aren't we supposed to forget what lies behind and strain toward what lies ahead? (Phil. 3:13)*

A This passage is not talking about burying past hurts, but about how Paul put his glorious past as an elite

Hebrew leader behind him and learned to be a humble disciple. He even dared to become an outcast in religious politics—you might say he was no longer interested in being a "looking-good kid."

Denying that someone hurt us is not the same as forgiving a hurt, although many prefer to substitute denial for forgiveness. To forgive someone, we must know the offense. Forgiveness is part of the healing process, described by the prophet Jeremiah: "You can't heal a wound by saying it's not there!" (Jer. 6:14, LB)

Q *When is anger appropriate?*

A The sin is not anger, but bitterness and actions that grow out of uncontrolled anger. When we let the sun go down on our wrath, we have not presented our anger to God. In His presence, we can sort out whether our anger comes from an appropriate source (others' hardheartedness, for example, Mark 3:5) or inappropriate source (our jealousy, for example, Gen. 4:1-8). Then we look at how we express anger. Being harsh, especially with those who are not involved, is inappropriate. We can learn to appropriately express our anger and to ventilate it using the tools discussed in Chapter 15.

Q *Isn't God powerful enough to heal us without dredging up our past?*

A Yes, God is the powerful healer of our afflictions and diseases. In some cases He may choose to do so instantly, but more often He works with us, teaching us and transforming us into His likeness through a slower process. This latter approach benefits us because the experience teaches us to know Christ better and to practice the skills of forgiveness.

Personal Reflection

Answer these questions as honestly as possible. Take a minute to quiet yourself before answering them and ask God to reveal to you anything that you need to know.

● What topics did your family avoiding talking about when you were growing up?

● Which person in your house did you trust most? Distrust the most?

● What feelings was your family uncomfortable with?

● Look at pictures of yourself as a child. What expression is on your face? Were you a happy child? What does it look as if you were thinking? What did you enjoy doing as a child? Were you a bubble blower? A fort builder? (Save these for use later.)

● If you have a friend with whom you could share these answers, whom would that be?

CHAPTER FIVE

Patterns that Block Our Growth

In an ideal world, children would grow up getting the love they need at all the right moments. During crises, parents or grandparents or teachers would pull them aside, tell them what they need to know and hold them on their laps as long as they need to be held. The reality is, however, that no parent fulfills every child's needs for love and security. It's easy to misread children, overreacting to minor troubles and never suspecting what does haunt them. Many parents do the best they can, but they become distracted with money problems and their own marital difficulties. Others imitate the harshness of their upbringing even though they desperately wish to do otherwise.

Jesus demonstrated the ideal version of childhood in which children feel safe and loved when He gathered them around Him and blessed them (Mark 10:13-16). When the disciples tried to push the children away, Jesus demanded to see them. He focused His full attention on them, listened to them, and touched them. He let them put their dirty little hands all over His tunic. His actions told the disciples that children are precious people worthy of His time. Like the best parent anyone could imagine, He intervened on the children's behalf and filtered out the negatives of the culture.

In our culture, however, it's been assumed that if children aren't being beaten, starved, or molested, they're fine. Yet many of us are not fine, considering the ways we need reassurance in the deepest parts of ourselves. *What must I do to feel loved?* Some of us find answers to that question by doing whatever it takes to please others or get their attention. These behaviors work against our goals as followers of Jesus.

The first step in shedding these destructive behaviors is to examine our upbringing and look for patterns of denial, blame, isolation and angry reactions. These four reactions are most apparent in families with these patterns.

A Parent or Sibling with "King Baby" Tendencies

A family member who acts like royalty, ruling the family and forcing his or her wishes on the others is sometimes called a "King Baby." Even though this person is an adult, he or she acts like a baby, demanding to have his or her needs met. These King or Queen Babies upset the entire family if they don't get what they want (attention, power, or even sympathy) or don't have access to whatever satisfies their drivenness (a job, money, or alcohol). The spouse and children put that parent or sibling's needs before their own. To a greater or lesser degree, King or Queen Baby parents and siblings dominate the other family members. They may not even be viewed this way because they also go out of their way to make up for their childish behavior by buying presents, doing kindnesses, and being fun.

This King Baby role may have developed over several generations. Perhaps Grandma pretended to be sick when she didn't get her way. Or Grandpa demanded that everyone shut their mouths whenever tension rose in the family. In these ways, they maintained control over family members. This controlling behavior passes to the next generation as their child (your parent) becomes a workaholic or tyrant-parent.

Many "King Baby" parents are alcoholics, yet their children don't realize it because alcohol is widely used in our society. Psychologist Claudia Black didn't realize her father was an alcoholic until she enrolled in a class on alcoholism as part of her training. Sure, he drank, but she had not realized how regularly. One in three families reports alcohol abuse by a family member[1] and Dr. Black guesses that 40% of those who have grown up in alcoholic homes don't realize that their mother or father was an alcoholic.[2] Alcoholism can affect several generations. The family of Donna, the church secretary profiled in Chapter 2, illustrates this. Donna's father, the child of an alcoholic, didn't drink but he adopted the alcoholic King

King Baby: a family member who acts like royalty

Baby disposition of his father. Eventually, Donna adopted it too.

King Baby parents who aren't alcoholic usually depend on something to satisfy their drivenness such as sugar, salt, caffeine, cigarettes (substances), or working too hard, volunteering at church programs, spending money, watching television, gambling, using pornography, or having affairs (activities). For example, some King Baby parents are addicted to rage. Eric's parents were strict church-goers and blew up at the most unpredictable moments. On the way to church, they could have a huge spat, screaming at the kids and blaming them for unrelated problems. Then when they turned into the church parking lot, it became quiet. His parents waved at friends and smiled as they got out of the car. Eric never knew what to expect from these rage-aholic parents.

In some families, a King Baby situation is unwillingly created through divorce, sickness, or mental illness. Family life revolves around nurturing a lonely single parent or a parent who is chronically ill. The children don't get the nurturing they need, but are expected to be the nurturing ones.

Caretakers

In a family with a "King Baby," the other parent and children put up with and even pamper "King Baby." They are the caretakers, and their payoff is that they're perceived as the "nice guys" of the family. They smooth things over, they negotiate with King Baby, they instigate whatever lying or sneaking around is necessary to avoid upsetting King Baby.

Here's how a caretaking spouse typically feels:

I love my husband, but I can't stand him. He keeps our family in an uproar so it's my responsibility to calm everyone. I pretend it doesn't bother me and I help my children get over the upsets.

Before he gets home, we scurry to pick things up

*and make sure his green Lazy-boy chair is in ex-
actly the right spot and free of toys. Then we tiptoe
around him after he arrives. I try to protect my
children by not letting them bring friends home.
They'll be embarrassed if their dad and I fight or if
he starts yelling at them to redo their chores.*

*Sometimes I wonder if his outbursts are my fault.
If I were a better housekeeper or a better lover, his
needs would be satisfied. Other times, I see that he's
a wonderful man and I'm glad I'm sticking it out.
When he's happy, we're happy. When he's miserable, we're miserable.*

The children pick up the caretaking parent's cues and
soon the entire family focuses their attention on pleasing
and protecting King Baby. On another level of awareness,
however, caretaking spouses don't like being controlled
by the King Baby and they retaliate by trying to control
the kids. "Stop that arguing right now or you'll turn out
like your father," they might say to children engaged in
normal childhood squabbles.

To escape the tiresome routine of nurturing the King
Baby parent, caretaking spouses often wrap themselves
in their own escapes. They may numb themselves with
food, TV, or romance novels, which causes them to be
unfocused and not fully present for the children. Eventually, they become addicted to stress and feel themselves
drawn to work situations and friendships in which chaos
is always going on. People ask them, "Why do you keep
working in that awful place?" Or, "Why do you let your
friend treat you that way?" They do it because chaos has
now become normal and they thrive on it. When parents
become preoccupied in this way, the child doesn't get
adequate attention from either parent.

Being a caretaker means we believe that if we put
enough energy into something or someone, we can fix
them. Jan saw this in herself:

*When we took some inner-city neighborhood kids
to a camp, I chose to teach the junior high group*

because they were the most difficult. I worked hard to develop creative, entertaining lesson plans, but two boys wouldn't cooperate no matter what. I had to separate them from the group every day, which broke my heart because I wanted so much to reach them.

I blamed myself for this even when one of the counselors who knew these boys well said, "Hasn't it occurred to you that they just don't know how to behave? It isn't your fault. It's going to take more than a week of camp to reach them." His words seemed like heresy to me. If I just prayed harder, if I just planned better, wouldn't things be OK?

I gave myself to the kids so completely that week that I didn't spend time with the other counselors at night. I stayed with the kids all the time. By Thursday night, I burned out. I sat outside in the dark crying and looking in the dining hall at the other counselors having a good time — and refreshing each other. Why was I so hard on myself? I wondered. Ten more years of expecting too much of myself would pass before I would begin to understand that I was a caretaker. Only then did I realize that even though I meant well, my service was about me and how I could help others, not about being God's instrument.

It can be a shock to those of us who are caretakers to discover that we see ourselves as "little messiahs." Besides that delightful part of us that loves beauty, order, and wholeness and wants to help and mend, there's a tendency to believe that we have the power to alter attitudes and behaviors if we are clever enough, spiritual enough.

Poorly Bonded Parents

Every couple on earth struggles to build a loving marriage, but parents who adopt King Baby or caretaking roles find their road even more difficult. Because they don't truly encourage each other and build each other up, they spend little meaningful time together. When they do, they may fight or peacefully co-exist in a state of "cold war." In both cases, the parents are emotionally separated, if not legally divorced.

To make up for the poor marital relationship, they often use other people to meet their needs. The mother may lean on her mother or on her daughter instead of her husband for companionship. If a husband needs his self-worth built up, he may seek love and recognition from his daughter or his sister or his secretary. Children who are used this way by parents feel inappropriately important because they fill in the gaps in the marital relationship. It usually divides the parents even more. Here is a typical example.

Lisa wanted to plant a garden but her husband Ralph wasn't excited about it. When Jeff, her teenage son, got home from school, she told him about how his father was being uncooperative, as usual. Could Jeff help her with the tomato plants she bought?

Jeff stood there weighing the decision. He looked at the basketball in his hands — he had planned to play ball with his friends. He could tell his mom needed him though, and after all, she gave him money whenever he needed it. She defended him to his dad when he got in trouble. Jeff tossed away the basketball and went to help his mom.

When Ralph got home, Lisa rubbed it in that Jeff "had to" help her. Ralph only rolled his eyes. Jeff felt bad that his mother had used him this way, but he and his dad were miles apart anyway — what did it matter if his dad didn't like it?

Jeff suffered at the hands of both parents. His father ignored him and his mother leaned on him for support as she would a spouse. Jeff felt he owed his mother some attention since she built her existence around him. Since neither parent focused on Jeff's needs, he was, in a sense, raising himself.

These inappropriate roles also force kids to be a buffer or go-between for parents. Perhaps your father told you things he wanted your mother to know and figured that you would tell her. This round-about sort of communication becomes a habit among all the family members. Even when children become adults, it continues. Mom now tells you how your sister should get a better job. Your mother expects you to speak to your sister for her. Though it's often done to avoid hurting someone's feelings, it creates misunderstandings and strangles communication. It overburdens innocent bystanders with information (usually negative) they don't need to know.

Families in which parents continually work at bonding with each other illustrate the slogan: "The best thing a father can do for his children is love their mother." The parents communicate directly, they try to meet each other's needs and together they work at meeting their children's needs. Because parents support each other, they can work toward being fully present for their children.

When children from these families grow up and get married, they can imitate the skills needed to nourish a communicative, trusting marriage. Because children have watched their parents solve problems and laugh together, the parents "trained them up" in the way they should go without even trying. When children of poorly bonded parents grow up and get married, they don't have this training. Even when they're wise enough to try to act differently from their parents, they often end up imitating them anyway because they haven't learned to talk, trust or feel.

Inappropriate Role Models

Parents assuming the roles of King Baby or the caretaker act childishly—pouting, manipulating, throwing tantrums—and so kids grow up thinking that this babyish behavior is appropriate in adults. When mature behavior is displayed in such a home, it is often the children who display it. Role reversal is common. Kids comfort and soothe their parents.

At the age of ten, Tim began rescuing his mother.

One time my mom was lying on our old green couch crying and said, "I'm going to kill myself, Tim."

"No, Mom, don't!" I pleaded.

"Why shouldn't I?" she asked.

I was only in fifth grade and I didn't know what to say. I looked through the doorway into the kitchen. The oven door was open and I thought of a reason that made sense to me: "You make great pizza, Mom. You put all that gooey cheese on it."

She smiled. She lay there for a while and then got up and fixed dinner. I've helped her! I thought. I felt powerful that I could prevent my mother's suicide.

As a young adult, I sensed that my role was to take care of people as I had done with my mother. I became a pastor, clueless that I was listening to the voice of my broken childhood telling me that I should take care of others. I just thought I wanted to help people.

When my mother would become depressed, I would sometimes tease her and try to make her laugh. She would feel better for a while. Other times, she would still feel down. Then I felt as if I'd failed. I hadn't tried hard enough. I wasn't clever enough.

Eventually I felt as if her problems were my fault. Guilt permeated my life. Even when I became a Christian as a teen, I felt guilty before God. I felt that I had to perform by leading, teaching, singing. I had to do it all, compulsively. I worried that my salvation was slipping.

In this way, Tim's childhood set the tone for his life. As a pastor, he devoted his life to listening to people and offering pat solutions. He felt guilty when things went wrong at the church.

One result of role reversal is that children grow up too

fast. They aren't allowed to be kids. Tim is well loved in his church for his empathic manner in pastoral counseling. "I started counseling my mother when I was seven. Then I became the listener-counselor for all my teen friends. No wonder I became a pastor." The bad news for Tim, however, is that as a young pastor, he's already burned out. No matter how much he tries to help people, he never feels successful enough.

You May Be Wondering . . .

Q *The Bible says that we should serve each other (Gal. 5:13) and be kind and compassionate to each other (Eph. 4:32). Isn't that what the caretaking parent is doing?*

A The caretaking parent is performing the outward motions of service, but often the inner motives are askew. Christ-like service and tenderhearted interaction are motivated by selfless love in which we ask ourselves how we can best serve someone. Caretaking spouses are asking themselves how they can pacify the King Baby spouse so their lives can be more peaceful. Giving in to a bully does not serve that bully. True selfless love would risk enough to gently confront King Baby parents about their behavior.

The caretaking parent also allows the King Baby parent to take advantage so that the caretaker is overworked, overstressed, and used. Is it God's will to let others exploit us that way? The apostle Paul's words are blunt: "In fact, you even put up with anyone who enslaves you or exploits you or takes advantage of you or pushes himself forward or slaps you in the face" (2 Cor. 11:20).

Q *Codependency is a much-used word. What does it mean?*

A Codependency means taking care of others so that their needs are more important than my own. It may seem to be done out of selfless service, but more often it comes out of a belief that I am not important enough to God, to myself, or to anyone else that I should look after my needs. Often, the other person's needs are not addressed at all, only their wants. For example, a codependent wife may fret because her husband wants his supper served at 6 P.M. sharp. She needs to go to the doctor, but will not get home in time to have supper ready at the appointed time. So she sacrifices a legitimate need to go to the doctor to satisfy a demand for supper at an exact time. The primary question for the codependent is not, *What about my needs?* but, *How is it that God intends for me to meet others' needs and for my needs to be met?*

Q *If someone behaves like a King Baby and drinks, is that person an alcoholic?*

A It's difficult to tell because many alcoholics are "looking-good kids," displaying a respectable image that our culture doesn't associate with alcoholism. Because they don't lie drunk in the street, we assume they don't have a problem. Yet alcoholism afflicts 18 million people in the United States[3] and approximately 28 million Americans are children of alcoholics, with 7 million of them under 18 years of age.[4] Gretchen's story illustrates how easy it is to miss that a parent is an alcoholic.

A few friends in college attended support group meetings for adult children of alcoholics. When they told me their stories about drunken parents crashing their birthday parties, I thanked God that my parents weren't alcoholics.

One time they mentioned that they were learning that children of alcoholics often create chaos wherever they go. They explained that they don't mean to do this but they're so used to chaos from their upbringing that they constantly stir things up. I thought about how true that was for me. I like to shock people, to make things seem worse than they are. If I'm getting along OK with a boyfriend, I start a fight just to get a little drama going. It's as if I'm an excitement junkie.

As they talked, I wanted to melt into my chair. Never had anyone diagnosed my problem so clearly. I felt as if a huge spotlight were shining on me. Could this be why I had so many relationship problems?

I made an excuse to leave. My mind raced. I was sure my dad wasn't an alcoholic. He drank beer, but never drank hard liquor. He hung out in bars, but he was a brilliant man and had held several high-paying positions. Of course, he was fired from his last job for losing his temper too many times.

Later that day, I told my friends I would go with them to their meeting "only so I wouldn't be so bored when they talked about it." There I read a pamphlet with a quiz from Johns Hopkins University that helps alcoholics identify themselves. I answered the twenty questions from my dad's point of view. He scored a "9," well beyond the count of those who "definitely have a problem with alcohol."

I remembered more about his drinking. I had seldom seen him drunk, but he talked about drinking all the time. We couldn't go anywhere that he didn't drink or get antsy for a drink. We used to carry beer in the trunk of our car all the time. I'm shocked to think that he could be an alcoholic—I thought that people dressed in business suits were OK.

Personal Reflection

Answer these questions as honestly as possible. Take a minute to quiet yourself before answering them and ask God to reveal to you anything that you need to know.

● If you had been one of the children Jesus put on His lap, what question do you think you would have asked Him?

● If there was a King Baby member of your family, what part of his or her behavior did you dread the most? How do you react today to people who remind you of that person?

● What steps could you take to begin to discover whether your good deeds flow out of a desire to serve selflessly, or out of a caretaking role motivated from keeping the peace or feeling good about yourself?

● If it was your experience that you took care of either of your parents, how do you think that affects you today?

● Pick one or two of the questions above and share your answers with a trusted friend. If you can't think of anyone, pray that God will begin to bring someone into your life with whom you can discuss the answers to these reflection questions. Or, perhaps you could attend a group — a discussion group, a discipleship group, or a support group — and share your answers with that group.

The questionnaire that Gretchen used is called "Are You An Alcoholic?" and reads this way:

ARE YOU AN ALCOHOLIC?	YES	NO
1. Do you lose time from work due to drinking?	___	___
2. Is drinking making your home life unhappy?	___	___
3. Do you drink because you are shy with other people?	___	___
4. Is drinking affecting your reputation?	___	___
5. Have you ever felt remorse for drinking?	___	___
6. Have you gotten into financial difficulties as a result of drinking?	___	___
7. Do you turn to lower companions and an inferior environment when drinking?	___	___
8. Does your drinking make you careless of your family's welfare?	___	___
9. Has your ambition decreased since drinking?	___	___
10. Do you crave a drink at a definite time daily?	___	___
11. Do you want a drink the next morning?	___	___
12. Does drinking cause you to have difficulty sleeping?	___	___
13. Has your efficiency decreased since drinking?	___	___
14. Is drinking jeopardizing your job?	___	___
15. Do you drink to escape from worries or trouble?	___	___
16. Do you drink alone?	___	___
17. Have you ever had a complete loss of memory as a result of drinking?	___	___
18. Has your physician ever treated you for drinking?	___	___
19. Do you drink to build up your self-confidence?	___	___
20. Have you ever been to a hospital or institution on account of drinking?	___	___
TOTAL	___	___

If you answer yes to any one of the questions, that is a definite warning that you may have a problem with alcohol. If you say yes, to any two, chances are you have a problem. If you answer yes to three or more, you definitely have a problem with alcohol.

CHAPTER SIX

The Way Families Tend to Be

There's usually one family in every church that we consider something of a "first family." Surely they don't have problems. But considering how the families of the giants of the faith struggled (both Abraham and Isaac offered their wives to Egyptian rulers), we can expect the best of families to have flaws. The following characteristics of families illustrate what happens when people react heavily with denial, blame, isolation, and angry actions to protect themselves.

Inconsistent Discipline and Love

If parents are distracted enough, children can break the same rules two days in a row and be punished one day but ignored the next. What's good on Tuesday is bad on Wednesday. They never know how their parents will react, so they check the tension barometer immediately when they walk in their house. Tony tells his experience.

My mom was stressed out that day, but I didn't know it. Like most other nine year olds, I couldn't let a creamy pan of fudge harden on the counter without sampling some of it. So I swooped my finger down the side of the pan while my mom was looking in the refrigerator.

She wheeled around and yelled, "Tony, how many times do I have to tell you not to do that?" Then she grabbed my hair and tugged hard.

I stood there stunned. My cheeks stung and my scalp throbbed. I fled to my room. I knew I didn't deserve such a harsh punishment.

An hour later, my dad came to me and said, "You need to understand that your mother is under a lot of stress. Don't be too hard on her. Try not to upset her."

Even as a child, I knew my mom was wrong for pulling my hair. I knew my dad shouldn't have excused her and put the responsibility on me to understand her. My mom should have apologized. Yet how could I complain? My dad and mom were the minister and his wife.

Sometimes my parents could be neat people, but I never knew what would set my mom off. On another day if I had swiped a finger full of fudge, she might have laughed and rumpled my hair.

In our culture, you show love based on how you feel that day, not on consistency or commitment. If parents' lives are going well or their children have made them proud, they show love to their children. If the parents are upset or their children have disobeyed, the parents are preoccupied or distant. In this setting, children feel insecure and unsure about what might happen. If parents are continually distracted by emotional difficulties, this inconsistent love and discipline become an insecure way of life.

Yet steady love and discipline are signs of near perfection, a mark all parents fall short of at some time. In families who live closer to that goal, children know to expect reasonable consequences for wrong behaviors and can count on parents to be fair. Parents accept their children's mistakes and communicate that they love their children no matter what. Then the whole family can pick up and move on.

Inappropriately Expressed Feelings

While some parents hold their feelings tightly in check, others express emotions in extremes. They praise too lavishly (relishing in ecstasy over a neighbor child who brings them the newspaper) or criticize profusely (lecturing the entire family for days about a tool left out in the rain). This spills over into the children's relationship with God and they imagine Him to have these same extreme mood swings.

Unpredictable outbursts scare the entire family, including the offending parent himself or herself. Family members develop such an even tone that when someone risks expressing deep feelings, their words are either ignored or denied, with the statement, "You shouldn't feel so unhappy. It's nothing."

Children need to express their feelings, especially feelings of fear. Otherwise, they feel hopeless that they'll ever get their needs met and may escape into snacking, watching TV, or taking drugs. As "hope deferred makes the heart sick" (Prov. 13:12), they face despair and depression as adults, but don't know why.

Violated Boundaries

Sometimes parents invade their children's space and dominate their world. They build their life around their children and become entangled in their children's relationships. As children grow older, parents can't let go of them. Ruth Ann's parents have always controlled her life, and she is struggling to find her independence.

> *I've asked my mother to give me some space. She calls me and gives me advice—get this job, buy this sofa, move closer. What really bothers me is that sometimes I ask for her advice. When I don't, I find myself thinking, Now, what would Mom tell me to do?*
>
> *I rely too much on my parents. I had an acci-*

dent last year and my car was towed to a gas station. I didn't tell my parents because I was trying to be independent, but I didn't call the insurance company either. I couldn't figure out what to do—my parents had always done those things for me. Besides, they had given me the down payment for the car (and chosen the exact car, of course). What would they say about the wreck?

Finally, they figured out I was riding the bus and they quizzed me about my car. My dad called the insurance company and went to the gas station to check on my car. I hate to admit that I was relieved. It scares me to think that I subconsciously put off doing anything because I knew that if I waited long enough my parents would bail me out.

This violation of boundaries happens for various reasons. One is that the parents have little sense of their God-given purpose in life and they try to live through their children. They're starved for meaningful relationships and seek intimacy from their children. They put all their emotional eggs in the baskets of their children.

Some parents violate children's boundaries with sexual or physical abuse. (One in three women and one in five men have been sexually abused.[1]) After a while, these children think that being a victim is normal and they expect others to treat them poorly. They often become the object of school yard bullies and teachers who subtly violate their sexual boundaries with inappropriate speech and conduct.

Children whose boundaries have been violated often struggle as adults, letting others make their choices and choose their friends. They don't know how to be responsible and independent and often gravitate to authoritarian churches that tell members in exact terms how to behave.

Others who have been enmeshed with their parents react by developing boundaries that are too rigid. They don't want their boundaries violated ever again so they erect thick walls of granite around themselves. They don't let anyone into their lives to connect with them, to influence them, to care for them.

This violation of boundaries, like the other tendencies in this chapter, strays far from the biblical model that urges parents to understand that children have limits and to respect those limits. Paul warned fathers (and it applies to mothers and other caregivers) not to "exasperate" or "embitter [their] children, or they will become discouraged" (Eph. 6:4; Col. 3:21). It's that healthy caution in parents that keeps them from lording their authority over their children. Parents moving toward these goals respect their children's privacy and knock on bedroom doors before they enter. They want the best for their children, but they don't live through them.

Lack of Communication

"That's not something our family talked about," is a common phrase that applies to conversations about sex, money, or the disease Grandpa really died of. If children ask questions about these topics, they are told they don't need to know the answers. Children find mom crying in her bedroom, but she tells them that nothing is wrong. Aunts and uncles may be living in an asylum or siblings may have died in childbirth, but children aren't told these things. Parents are often trying to protect children, but it amounts to denial because children pick up the latent sadness and assume they are the cause.

Keeping so many topics underground means that conversations are full of codes and hidden meanings. People tend to speak passively or aggressively, but not with assertiveness.

Passive Communication	Aggressive Communication	Assertive Communication
you say nothing about what you want or need	you scream about what you need or want	you express needs and wants in a calm, direct manner

Open, honest communication teaches children to speak the truth in love (Eph. 4:15). They learn that even when they don't have good feelings about others, they can speak up without blowing up. They can ask questions and make observations in a gentle way. Children see that parents can admit their mistakes even though it makes them vulnerable. This helps kids know that they too will make mistakes and survive.

Closed System Mentality

In families with an "open system," children get close to other people. They invite other children over to play and they have adult friends such as youth group sponsors or scout leaders. The parents have nothing to hide and are eager to grow as people. To use a term from the study of cell biology, the family acts as a "semi-permeable membrane" with new healthy ideas flowing in and out.

When families exhibit a "closed system" mentality, they don't welcome new information or ideas. Children know by example not to get close to anyone, especially adults, outside the family. Parents stick with what they've always believed and don't want to hear about books or groups on parenting. This closed system also means that families are careful not to let information out either. They keep family secrets about whatever the latest drama at home might be and about parents' unusual behaviors.

Tension

The stage for poor development is set from infancy if King Baby parents are wrapped up in their own tensions to the point that they don't pick up their babies tenderly. Instead, they may shove them on to the changing table, yank off the diaper, and jerk on a the new one. Even these little ones pick up tense emotional messages. This tension robs kids of their childlike tendencies to be adventuresome, playful, and curious. It's as if they skip basic classes in life—Childhood 101 and 102—and are thrust into adulthood prematurely. One way they cover up this tension is by acting like "looking-good kids."

As adults, nervousness abounds. They work at pleasing others and appearing perfect. They try to act like they think adults should act, but end up faking it emotionally. There's little time or energy left for seeking God.

Low Self-worth

Sometimes children are exasperated or embittered because parents don't affirm them and they never feel a sense of accomplishment. A parent might even admonish a child who was honored at school: "Now, don't get a big head about this, OK?" Some parents belittle or criticize children because they think this causes children to try harder. They don't realize that those small words of encouragement—"Good job!"—are the building blocks to a child's sense of achievement. Without this, children become adults who lack confidence to fulfill the goals and dreams God puts within them.

Other times, children develop a low opinion of themselves because their parents say nothing. Parents may stay detached because they're so engulfed in their problems or because they don't feel confident as parents. They don't know how to hug or discipline their children and they're afraid they'll make mistakes so they don't try. Still other parents don't attach to their children because children aren't a high priority in their lives. The children essentially raise themselves.

If parents' moods vary greatly, so does the child's desire to achieve. Danielle remembers her childhood—and her self-worth—being full of ups and downs.

When my dad was working and my mother was happy, I could give speeches at school or try out for drill team. I was confident and tried hard. When my dad was in one of his angry moods and my mom cried a lot, I changed. I didn't call my friends or study very hard. I looked for reasons to get out of the house. Many times I jumped on my bike and rode out into the country. The wind blew against my face and dried the tears. I felt like two people most of the time. Sometimes I was outgoing and carefree; other times I was scared and tired. I longed to grow up and get away.

When I went off to college, I was afraid at first, but then I started talking to people and getting involved. My teachers and supervisors rarely came down on me but when they did, they were calm about it. I felt like a living, breathing person for the first time.

This is not to say that self-worth for the Christian is based on one's own accomplishments. Our self-worth is based on God's unwavering love for us. The answer to that core question—*What must I do to feel loved?*—is nothing. We already are loved by God, but translating that to a child is a tricky thing because children want to see and touch the arms of God. Consistent, loving actions in the adults around them make it easier.

Delayed Development

Growing up in a chaotic family can affect emotional, intellectual, and social development. For example, children from alcoholic families experience more distress in moods, conformity, relationships, leadership skills, and emotional stability.[2] Still other studies show an increase of depression,[3] hyperactivity,[4] aggression,[5] self-esteem,[6] and legal difficulties as children and adults.[7]

Stress makes it difficult for children to reach their intellectual potential too. In a recent study on how stress affects the brain, researchers found that subjecting rats to hormones associated with stress for long periods of time worked against their brain's ability to learn and remember.[8] That may explain why kids can't concentrate when their parents are arguing. They stop doing their math homework to listen. *What are they arguing about this time?* they wonder. *Will they get a divorce? If they do, will I live with Mom or Dad?* They're so distracted, they miss the math principles that are foundational for the next quarter.

Stress also affects the way children's personalities develop. For example, psychoanalyst Erik Erikson observed that children specialize in learning certain developmental tasks during specific stages of life. Here is a simplified version of how those tasks and stages correspond.[9]

STAGES OF LIFE	DEVELOPMENTAL TASKS	
	Positive	Negative
Infancy (0-2)	Trust	Mistrust
Toddlerhood (2-4)	Autonomy	Shame & Doubt
Early School age (5-7)	Initiative	Guilt
Middle School (8-12)	Industry	Inferiority
Adolescence (13-22)	Identity	Alienation

It's possible that when children experience trauma during one of these stages, they don't develop the corresponding developmental task as fully as they should. If a temporary crisis occurred in your family (your mother's father died and she withdrew in grief for a year or so) when you were six, you may find that you lack initiative. Depending on when negative childhood experiences occurred, you may be lacking to some degree in:

- trust (having confidence in others' integrity, ability and good will)
- autonomy (feeling comfortably independent)
- initiative (becoming self-starters)
- industry (working hard, finishing tasks)
- identity (feeling like we know and like who we are).

These developmental tasks affect our spiritual life too. How can we develop a growing relationship with God if it's difficult to trust anyone? How can we avoid going along with the crowd when our sense of autonomy is diminished? How can we talk to a friend about God when our initiative is stunted? How do we finish a task when our sense of industry isn't developed? How do we seek God in choosing a career or spouse without a sense of identity? God is interested in our learning these developmental tasks because they are part of how we respond to Him, to others, and the world. Carolyn's story illustrates this:

Carolyn is struggling in her marriage. She wants to trust her husband and he senses that she is holding back and questioning his motives constantly. When Carolyn discussed this with her counselor, he asked about her infancy. Carolyn recalled that her parents were divorced when she was an infant, so she questioned her mother and found out that her mother and father argued a lot during that time. The subsequent silent treatment they gave each other extended to her as well.

Carolyn's therapist noted that this could be one of several reasons why Carolyn developed a limited and inconsistent sense of trust. Like a newly blossoming flower that has been walked on, Carolyn still grew but was wounded. Other growing up experiences also taught her not to trust until, now as an adult, her sense of trust is limited. She wants to make her marriage work, but it is a great struggle because of her lack of trust.

Identifying areas of struggle is not a license to blame parents, but to give us a place to begin to seek God's healing in our lives.

Glimpses of Grace

An open family system allows children a glimpse of how other families live. Children are shocked when they stay overnight with friends and find out that other families talk and laugh. They can barely understand a world that is so genuinely peaceful or fun. They often reach out to these friends to find more proper boundaries in life — what's too personal, what's offensive.

Other times, a relative or neighborhood family will take a child under their wing, taking them places and having them in their home. When children experience this healthy family interaction, it whets their appetites to do things differently. They make comments such as, "When I grow up, I'm going to be just like. . . ." Little do they know that their bodies and their memories are set up so that they will probably repeat the behaviors they learned in their family unless they undergo a process of self-examination and learn new tools for surrendering to God.

You May Be Wondering . . .

Q *If I'm nothing like my "King Baby" parent, none of this affects me, right?*

A Most of us try to become the opposite of our King Baby parent. We may not have the same outward behaviors (hot temper, demanding tone of voice), yet we have the same inner drives, sadness, and anger that we keep safely hidden under a calmer demeanor. Or, instead of being critical and authoritarian, we respond by being weak and permissive. The family system affects all its members, although they respond differently according to their personality and what roles are left to them in the family (see Chapter 7). It's as if we are changing chairs on the Titanic — we all participate in the same problem, only from a different perspective.

Q *I get frustrated with my kids. Does this mean I have a problem?*

A It's normal to have good and bad days with children. Nobody's perfect. What matters is the frequency and severity of the anger. Are you a parent who disciplines by giving consequences instead of ventilating anger? When parents do act in anger but then admit their mistakes, they show their children how they face their failures and they usually earn their children's respect.

Q *My parents didn't compliment or encourage me. How could this be affecting me now?*

A Children develop initiative and industriousness when they are complimented on what they do right and are not ridiculed when they make mistakes. In this culture, parents tend to criticize children when they make mistakes. Parents can reflect God's love when they encourage children whether they succeed or fail. This teaches them that trying is what is important, not winning or losing.

Lack of encouragement in childhood affects us as adults because we judge ourselves harshly. We become perfectionists, trying to prove that we are good enough. Instead, we need to build relationships in which we are accepted and in which we can fail without being condemned.

Q *What if I can't remember anything about my childhood?*

A One way to start is to watch children play. Go to a park and watch how simple, teachable, and trusting children are. Ask yourself, *What's my earliest positive memory? My earliest negative one? Did I have a pet? What sounds do I remember?*

It's important not to do this in isolation. Show your childhood pictures to others and tell them what you were like. (If your childhood was particularly painful, you may need a therapist to help you manage the fears that come with this.) Within the heart of that child in the picture are great hopes and perhaps even blossoming qualities that have been stamped out. If it was God who planted them, He can help you recover them.

Personal Reflection

Answer these questions honestly. Take a minute to quiet yourself before answering them and ask God to reveal to you anything that you need to know. If you're participating in a group or sharing answers with a friend, pick out the questions you feel comfortable answering in the group.

● Would you say that you tend to be passive, aggressive, or assertive? (See the chart on page 74.) Perhaps you behave differently in different situations.

● Name a situation in which you would like to become more assertive — stating your needs and wants in a calm, direct manner.

● Write a paragraph or two about how you think the people in that situation would respond. (Perhaps you'd like to buy a journal or dig out an old spiral notebook in which to write your thoughts.)

● Do you sometimes feel that God has mood swings? How do you think your answer is related to *your* life and growing up in your family?

● Who were the adults outside your family who affected you most — for good or bad? How did they help or hurt your development of trust, independence, initiative, industry, or sense of identity?

● With what kind of people are you most comfortable? Why do you think that is? Does it have anything to do with your childhood?

● Look at pictures of yourself as a child (Use the same ones used in Chapter 5.) Do you see blossoming qualities God put within you that may have been stamped out for some reason? Ask God to show you those parts of yourself that have been missing for a long time.

CHAPTER SEVEN

Roles that Get Us through Childhood

The Wells family are pillars of the church. They attend every service and can always be counted on to help. Dad is a ruddy-complexioned mail carrier who serves on the church board. Mom, tall and erect, is a teacher and directs the Vacation Bible School every year.

Even though they have the same values and are both interested in church, they aren't warm toward each other. Mom often objects to decisions made at church and tells Dad how he ought to change them. "I'm not a wave maker," he often tells her, but then he makes a few waves at church to appease her.

Their oldest child, *Melissa,* follows her mother's example. She cleans the house every Saturday and she began teaching Sunday school when she was twelve. Melissa makes excellent grades in high school and holds an office in student government. She keeps the other Wells kids in line when her parents attend church meetings at night.

David, the second child, has never liked school. He doesn't like Melissa and tells her she acts like an old lady. David makes jokes about the conflict he hears behind his parents' closed bedroom doors. He is disgusted by Dad's blind obedience to Mom. A few years ago David's friends began wearing gang-style clothes and carrying knives.

David did the same—it looked like a good way to be his own person. It causes confrontations with his parents, but he likes these fights. "At least they take off their Christian masks," says David.

Cindy, the second daughter, also hears all the commotion behind closed doors, but drops out. Everyone says that Cindy is shy and sweet, but she has few friends. She doesn't bring those few girlfriends around because Mom is so controlling. Cindy stays in her room a lot, drawing. She did speak up once to ask for a puppy, but Mom wouldn't let her have one because she said that dogs were loud and messy. Dad gave Cindy a parakeet, which she babies and keeps in her room.

Gary, the youngest, sees the hurt ricocheting back and forth among Mom, Dad and David, and does what he can to make things better. He often defends his dad, and once when Dad brought up divorce, Gary spent the evening talking him out of it. Gary likes to ride alone in the car with Dad because they get a chance to talk.

Children look for ways to get their parents' attention (or to avoid negative attention) and without realizing it, they develop a role in their family. It gives them a sense of consistency, predictability and security. Regrettably, they often become anchored in this role and as adults they become people they don't like very much. The Wells children adopted the following roles.[1]

The Responsible Child
In the midst of chaos,
I'll work hard so people will love me.

The oldest child is often responsible anyway, but in a family full of denial, blame, isolation, and angry outbursts, it's doubly so. Also called "the hero," the Responsible child takes care of younger brothers and sisters as Melissa does. Sometimes responsible children even take care of the parents. At the age of ten, they can tuck an alcoholic parent in bed and make dinner for the whole family.

These responsible ones are seven going on twenty-seven. Their typical day includes getting an A on a test, helping the teacher after class and doing the laundry when they get home. Parents are proud of this "banner child" for being so mature. If families like the Wells are advised to seek counseling, they object: "How can you say our family has problems? Look at Melissa. She's a 4.0 student. She's a cheerleader. She's involved in church. Could a problem family produce a child like this?"

When these children become adults, they may not want to raise a family of their own. Suzanne, the Responsible child in an alcoholic family, mothered two younger sisters (both of whom got pregnant as teens) and a younger brother who committed suicide. Before she married, she warned her fiance', "I'm not having children. I already raised one set of kids and they turned out bad."

In the work place, responsible adult children are successful, but insecure. They may be rigid and controlling with very little insight into why they do what they do. *Somebody's got to organize the world,* they think. *So I will.* Tragically, they take the job and they spend their lives proving themselves.

The Acting Out Child
In the midst of chaos,
I'll become the problem so people will notice me.

These children misbehave and act out the hidden pain of their family. As a result, they are often the presenting problem when their family comes to counseling. Because the family views David as the problem and don't understand that their family has a problem, this role is also called the "scapegoat." When the counselor asks the Wells family what a typical night at home is like, David delivers the straight scoop about how no one is allowed to say what they really think or feel. It's no surprise that this child is considered the black sheep of the family.

The family doesn't realize that Acting Out children run

away, starve themselves, get pregnant or wreck a car because of their desire to be known, loved, and accepted by their parents. Like the others, this child wants to know what it takes to feel loved and has concluded that positive attention isn't possible, so he or she gets into trouble, thinking that negative attention will feed the hunger.

As adults, Acting Out children are often excitement junkies. They move from relationship to relationship without attaching. They bore quickly and don't control their impulses or wait for things. They enjoy new and changing environments so they migrate from place to place never finding home.

Their typically low tolerance for frustration makes

Understanding the roles we played in our families helps us figure out why we treat others the way we do

them self-destructive. Of all the children, they're most likely to become alcoholic or chemically dependent. Yet they have the best chance of working through their past issues because they didn't participate in the denial of the family. They can name their problems and seek help.

The Adjuster
In the midst of chaos,
I'll tune people out so they won't bother me.

Some children get burned too many times early in life and never venture out again. They adjust their expectations because they've learned they won't get their needs met. "Why try?" is their motto.

Adjusters usually detach from their family to become the "lost" children. In the Wells family, Cindy detaches by staying in her room and playing with her parakeet. She's also good at drawing, which is a fitting hobby because it gives her a world to which she can withdraw. She can detach even in the presence of the family as she watches TV and never hears the undercurrents of tension around her. To them, she is invisible.

When Adjusters grow up, it's difficult for them to live with other people and feel safe. They may stay uninvolved in their family. They have tuned out for so long that it's difficult to tune back in, to feel comfortable.

Adjusters often reproduce their family environment and marry someone who keeps their lives in an uproar. If situations become too troubled, they do what they've always done: leave. That may mean going from marriage to marriage or from church to church or from job to job looking for a place to feel comfortable.

The Placater
In the midst of chaos,
I'll make people feel better so they'll love me.

Placaters act as comforters, referees, and even counselors for the family. They're hypersensitive to the feelings of other people and read people well. They try to solve problems as Gary Wells does. When Mom becomes upset with Dad, Gary listens to her complaints and then pleads Dad's case to her. His placater role has become so established that the other family members come to him with problems.

Some Placaters "fix" their families by getting them to laugh. This version of a placater is called the "mascot" or "family clown." When the Wells family gets particularly tense, Gary entertains his mother and sisters by coming up with ridiculous ways of taking out the kitchen garbage. If David storms out, Gary distracts his family with a funny story about school.

As adults, Placaters often become caretakers. They get walked on by others and they sacrifice themselves to the point that they neglect their own needs. Other people lean on Placaters so hard that they often blame the Placaters when things go wrong. "That's what you told me to do and it didn't work!" they say. The vintage Placater takes the blame.

They may complain about this but do little about it because they think this is their lot in life. If they get into relationships in which people want to meet their needs, it feels foreign to them. They may even leave these healthy relationships because they're unable to adjust.

Three of these four roles are "looking-good kids," which explains why so many families with undercurrents of denial, blame, isolation, and anger seem otherwise. The Responsible children keep the peace, Adjusters find their own peace and Placaters negotiate peace, while the Acting Out children disturb the peace.

These three looking-good kid roles are also susceptible to perfectionism. A Responsible child is obsessed with doing perfectly as adults the kinds of things they did as children—achieving in school (work), keeping the house tidy, caring for children. Placaters beat themselves up when they can't heal everybody's hurts. Adjusters are less concerned with perfectionism, except in their area of escape. Cindy Wells, for example, has to draw each picture perfectly or she rips it up. Athletes have to reach certain milestones every time, scoring a touchdown every time.

Uncovering The Real Me

Understanding the roles we played and still play helps us figure out why we treat other people the way we do and misunderstand promptings from God if they conflict with our role. Acting Out kids don't adjust or try to be responsible; Placaters and Adjusters don't speak out.

Figure out what role(s) you played

You may feel that you fit primarily into one role and secondarily into another. Some children, especially only children, may absorb a little of all the roles or use two at the same time. John, whose father was a doctor, was a responsible child at home, at church, and at school with one group of kids. He had another set of friends at school, with whom he played the role of acting out child by taking drugs. His family was never found out and he grew up to be a looking good responsible adult who nurses a secret love of pornography as his way of acting out.

What if you don't remember what role you played? It may not be obvious at first. Listen to the stories your family tells you. Perhaps you'll recognize which roles your siblings played and then you'll see yourself. Discovering the role you played may shock you. It's similar to hearing your voice on audio tape for the first time. *Is this me?* you ask.

Determine how you're still playing your role

The logical conclusion is that once children leave home they shed their roles because they don't need them anymore. That isn't how it works.

As adults, we use our childhood roles on our jobs, in

our churches and in our families. Our new life situations may not require this of us but we feel comfortable in these roles. We have carved these niches for ourselves and we become stuck there. Here's how Dan did this.

Fifteen years ago, my father almost died of cirrhosis of the liver. My three older sisters and I sat for many long hours by his bedside in the hospital. He barely made it through the ordeal. Throughout this stressful time, I, a placater, acted as the family counselor. I listened to my sisters. I reassured one sister that she hadn't failed my dad. I told another how well she had taken care of me. I cheered the youngest one up by telling her all the great qualities she had that were like my dad. I patted myself on the back for being so caring when I felt so bad.

After my sisters and I took Dad home, my sisters seemed at peace, but I felt keyed up inside. I went to the gym and played basketball extra hard. The sweat rolled down my back and my socks were soaked. I ran to the shower room.

Alone in the shower, my feelings overcame me. What if my father had died? I felt so afraid and so alone. I cried uncontrollably as I had never done before in my life. The noise of the shower barely covered up my sobbing. I felt like the way I felt as a little boy knowing my father was killing himself with alcohol. There was nothing I could do then; there was nothing I could do now.

I was crying for myself too. Where were my sisters when I needed them? As usual, they didn't know I was hurting because I couldn't share my sorrow with them. I wanted to talk to them and tell them how afraid I was, but I couldn't. That wasn't my role—I was the placater. I had to grieve by myself. That's when I realized that the placater role was becoming too lonely a road to follow.

Our roles hamper us in our relationships too. We can't stop playing our role with our spouse and friends. Responsible children often don't let their spouses carry their part of the load. Acting Out children want their spouses to carry it all. Adjuster children won't talk about problems with their friends and Placaters attempt to solve their friends' problems with simplistic solutions.

Question your role-like tendencies in everyday situations

Instead of acting on automatic pilot in our roles, we can establish ongoing conversations with God asking if we're behaving in certain ways because God is leading this way, or because that's what our role demands of us.

- The Responsible child asks God, *Am I helping this person because You, God, are leading me to do this? Or because it gives me the kudos I need to feel loved?*
- The Acting Out child asks God, *Am I creating a problem in my office because You have led me to see that someone needs to bring up this problem? Or because I know it will get people's attention?*
- The Adjuster asks God, *Am I backing off from this friendship because You have shown me how this person is blocking my relationship with You? Or because I'm scared to death to be close to her?*
- The Placater needs to ask God, *Am I listening sympathetically to this person because You have brought me into his life to be his friend? Or because "fixing" people makes me feel important?*

Understanding our childhood role is a life-long process of seeking God's will for our lives and making different behavior choices. We may even "test the waters" by responding to others outside our roles and then waiting to see if God shows us that is more appropriate. As soon as we recognize our role-like behavior, we may want to go back and correct it. As difficult as it was for Dan, he called his oldest sister when he got home and told her how broken he felt about his dad. He knew that she was the Responsible child of the family and would understand better than his other sisters how he tried to take care of people. He knew that she didn't understand everything he was saying, but it was important that he step out of his Placater role by sharing his grief with someone else.

As each of us uncovers our real selves, we talk to ourselves in a new way: *In the midst of chaos, I will ask God to show me how to behave in each situation and I will ask Him to help me do that.*

You May Be Wondering . . .

Q *Do children ever change roles?*

A Roles may change as the children grow up. In your early years, you might use one role and then another in your adolescent years. When the Responsible child leaves the nest, another child may fill that vacant spot.

Q *I think my boss is a Responsible child/Placater and I'm tired of the way she takes care of me. What can I do?*

A With as much serenity as you can muster, exert your independence. When she insists on telling you how something has to be done, you might say, "That works well for you, but I think I can do the job better if I do it this way." If she makes suggestions and offers counsel about your personal life, you might say, "Thanks for your concern. I'm considering other options, but I will also consider what you have said." Because you understand something of her entrapment in her role, you are well equipped to pray for her. This will also add some serenity to your frustration.

Q *What's wrong with being a perfectionist?*

A Striving to do the best you can is desirable. Like the apostle Paul, we "press on toward the goal to win the prize for which God has called [us] heavenward in

Christ Jesus" (Phil. 3:14). The issue is not the actions, but the motives and drivenness. The right motive for doing our best is our love for God. Our actions become perfectionistic at the moment where we are unable to accept that we have flaws. If we don't do it perfectly, we will not be loved by ourselves or God. There's little room for error. When we make a mistake, we can't recover from it because we're no longer lovable when we make mistakes. We're also being perfectionistic when our striving becomes a point of pride. At some place within us echoes the thought, *I always do things right. People look up to me because I do things right and so on.*

Q *How do I quiet my tendency to play my role and attempt to hear God better?*

A As we let go of the automatic pilot of our role-like behavior, every situation becomes an opportunity for seeking God and listening to Him. As we set aside the actions and words that our role calls forth from us, we can gain a sense of quiet. In that moment, it is easier to sense God's direction when we make choices.

That quiet can be difficult to obtain. Jan found her role so overbearing that she did the following.

As I listened to myself talk one evening in a support group, I became aware of how flippantly I gave advice and how easily I criticized people. I was a vintage Placater. From somewhere, I got the idea that I would try not to give advice or offer my opinion for thirty days and see what happened. I told the group this and even made myself accountable to them.

The next month was eerie. I pulled back from all the advice giving and criticizing, but I could still hear myself in my head. Many times I went off to be alone to sort out those thoughts and lay them before God. Would it have really helped that person if I had offered my observations? I often asked God. The most startling thing, though, was that in my outward silence, I found myself listening to people much more intently. I gained a greater empathy for them.

I have always believed that one of God's purposes for me is to encourage people, but now I see that my Placater behavior hampered me instead of helping me. I felt the need to solve everyone's problems by next Tuesday, at least, and I didn't truly offer the listening heart I can offer now.

Personal Reflection

Answer these questions as honestly as possible. Take a minute to quiet yourself and ask God to reveal to you anything that you need to know. If you're participating in a group or sharing answers with a friend, pick out the questions you feel comfortable answering in the group.

● Which role(s) feel familiar to you?

● In what ways might you say that your role has hampered you in relationships? In the work place? With God?

● How do you respond to yourself when you make a mistake? Place your response on the appropriate place on each continuum.

harsh impatience	gentle patience

a crisis to be weathered	a problem to be solved

● What steps could you take to set aside your role long enough to seek God's purposes for your life?

CHAPTER EIGHT

Scrambling to Be Adults

Can you imagine building cabinets and finding you have no hammer, no screwdriver, not even a saw? Or suppose you need to bake brownies, but you have no mix, flour or eggs? What's more, imagine that in both cases it's impossible to buy what you're missing. You have to substitute with what you have.

I can't! you protest. I don't have the right materials!

As adults, we face a similar predicament. We aren't fully prepared for adult life. Juan, for example, got a good education and now has a good job, but he can't process the criticisms he receives in his performance reviews. So he drifts from job to job. He works at being witty and he buys the right clothes, hoping to attract a wife, but he can't open up to others with his fears and doubts. He goes to church and attends Bible studies, but there's something missing in his faith he can't explain.

What was sown in his childhood comes to fruition as an adult:

CHILDHOOD		ADULTHOOD
denial	creates	distrust
blame	creates	self-condemnation
isolation	creates	alienation
repeated angry actions	create	tension

Distrust, self-condemnation, alienation, and tension force people into a corner in which they feel they must protect themselves. In that corner, vulnerability toward God and toward other people seems like an unattainable goal.

Distrust

Our culture urges people to pretend to be what they're not. Customer service personnel ask, "Can I help you?" when they would rather not. Advertisements try to persuade us that we can trust politicians, doctors, or self-help gurus to have all the answers, but they usually don't. If you add these influences to childhood patterns of denial, distrust develops. People protect themselves through the following means.

Overreacting to uncontrollable circumstances[1]

Hearing there's a new supervisor or being diagnosed with an obscure health problem can be a signal to assume the worst will happen. Flexibility seems impossible. Some of us find relationships unmanageable and unruly, so we become commandos, in effect. If someone attacks us verbally, we defend ourselves with a destructive verbal raid or an evasive maneuver.

The need to control is fueled by a desire to protect ourselves. If we've been hurt in the past, such as feeling left out from a social group or left in a love relationship, we want to avoid being hurt at all costs. We may use our roles to control people, placating the bully or tuning out the person who ignores us. It's frustrating to realize that no matter how hard we try, we can't make everything come out right. We can't make a spouse, children, boss, and employee willing to do what we want them to do.

Lying when it would be just as easy to tell the truth

Although Scripture clearly states that lying is wrong, bending the truth seems good to those who lied to protect themselves from a King Baby parent or sibling. As adults, they lie to stay out of trouble or they exaggerate their troubles to get attention. Ultra "looking-good kids" may even exaggerate their problems so they can impress others with how quickly they can solve them.

Keisha shows us an example of how open communication can be difficult.

While visiting a friend, I stayed in her sister's old room and found a beautiful pink scarf, which she had obviously discarded when she moved out years ago. I knew the scarf would look great with a dress I had just bought so I put it in my suitcase. I told myself that I would ask my friend later if I could have it.

Still, I was afraid to ask her. In my home growing up, I tried not to get my father riled up or bother my mother so I wasn't used to asking for things. I rehearsed what she would say to me: "I should probably ask my sister. I'll check and let you know." Then I would feel rejected. Or perhaps, she would say, "That old thing? Take it." Even though my friend is a generous, optimistic person, I couldn't risk even a small bit of rejection.

Making decisions based on whim or intense analysis

If you don't trust yourself to make wise decisions, you go to extremes in making them. One extreme is making decisions based on impulse and then regretting them. Sandra broke up with her long-time boyfriend after a few days of confused feelings. She didn't think it over because examining feelings is difficult and explaining them is even more difficult. She tried to apologize, but it didn't work.

After being burned from being impulsive, some move to the opposite extreme and become too analytical. They research decisions, juggling their desire to please, their self-criticism, and their over-responsibility. They feel stressed out from turning things over and over in their minds.

Working through distrust involves surrendering to God our fears of people and the need to protect ourselves. This flows out of an understanding that God has not abandoned us and that He will protect us. At the same time, we learn to trust a few people enough to tell them what we feel, what we want, what we think. It's such a relief to depend on others a little bit without having to figure everything out for ourselves.

Self-Condemnation
Judging ourselves without mercy

As our own worst critics, we give others a break but not ourselves. When we pick on ourselves this way, we expect, and even imagine, that others do the same. Brent began condemning himself as a child:

> *When I played games with other kids on my block and at school, I was too busy judging myself to enjoy games. I worried a lot about being overweight and how people might judge me. If we ran up a hill in P.E. class, I didn't think about reaching the top, because I was worried about how I looked to the guys behind me. If I heard someone laugh, I assumed they were laughing at me. If a guy breezed by me and slapped me on the back, I didn't listen to what he said because I was sure he was making fun of me. Even though I've lost weight, I'm still worried that I don't look right and that people are making fun of me.*

Some Christians mistakenly believe that being hard on themselves is the key to being better. Instead, harshness often deflates any belief that God can use them. This usually translates into judging others without mercy too. I may not say anything about how poor the other person's lawn looks or how much his children misbehave, but I notice every detail and tuck it away in my mind for judgment later.

Seeking approval and affirmation

All that unrelenting judgment leaves people in constant need of reassurance. Adults often transfer that need for approval from parents to friends, spouse, church leaders, or employers. That desire for approval makes us skilled at reading people. As children, we may have studied the King Baby parent's face—eye movement, quivering lips—so that now we sense details that others miss. We can tell what people are thinking—or think we can—just by their expressions. Hungering for affirmation leaves us open to considering everyone's opinion, but neglecting God, who tests our hearts.

Being loyal, even to hurtful people

Some who have grown up with a King Baby and caretaker parent find they have extreme loyalty to anyone they perceive as a caretaker. This may mean they stay in poor relationships and job situations when others would not. Belinda's story speaks to this problem:

Wherever I work, people dump on me. My boss cusses at me and tells me to find things he thinks I've lost. When I find them and it's obvious that he lost them, he doesn't apologize. He just says, "Oh, yeah."

Someone suggested that I quit. I can't quit because I keep thinking that I can change him, that I'm a good influence on him. Something inside me drives me to stick things out, no matter how hopeless they seem.

It's the same with my father. When I talk with him on the telephone, I let him say things about me that aren't true—exaggeration, innuendoes. The other day I stood up for myself when he blew some-

*thing out of proportion. He got mad and hung up.
I felt guilty for a week. I almost called him and
apologized except that I've promised my support
group that I won't. I'm practicing for the day I can
say to him, "I won't allow you to talk to me that
way."*

Throwing off self-condemnation means giving ourselves a break. We appreciate our progress, however
slow it may be. Focusing on God's great love for us and
what He leads us to do helps us worry less about pleasing others. We seek relationships and work situations in
which we are treated with fairness and respect.

Alienation
Feeling less adequate than others

Have you ever felt as if everybody else knows hidden
secrets about life? Sometimes it may look as if others
have fun and know where they're doing while you "wing
it" through life. For some, it seems as if everyone else is
getting the punch line of a joke and you aren't. Deep
inside, you may even be afraid that *you* are the joke.

If as a child, the adults around you communicated to
you in words, actions, or facial expressions that other
things were more important than you were, you may
believe in your heart that you aren't worth much even
though you would never put it into words. Perhaps these
adults didn't intend this, but they felt frustrated, rushed,
or hopeless in their own circumstances. When worthlessness becomes a familiar feeling, shame washes over us
even for small failures. This shame may cause us to distance ourselves from people so that others think we're
snobbish when we're actually afraid and intimidated by
them.

For some people, this shame stems from their parents'
embarrassing behavior. Sometimes it's unintentional because parents have immigrated from another culture.
Other times their embarrassing behavior flowed from

their addiction to rage or perfection or alcohol. Carlos talks about feeling less than others.

I was playing well in one of my high school basketball games when I saw my father come in. He's a really smart guy, but he's also opinionated and gets upset at games. I could tell by the way he walked that he was in one of his moods. I hoped he would sit down and be quiet, but he didn't. I kept watching him to make sure he didn't embarrass me in front of my friends. I didn't realize how nervous I was until I missed an easy shot out on the court.

My dad yelled out something and I looked around to see if people could tell he was my dad. I tried to stare straight ahead and keep playing, but I couldn't concentrate. Finally, I told the coach I felt sick so he would take me out. I couldn't take the pressure of worrying if my dad would embarrass me. That kind of thing happened often enough that I still tense up when I think someone's going to embarrass me. I never feel like one of the guys.

Struggling with intimate relationships

Having friends or being married doesn't necessarily guarantee that we have let anyone see the interior of ourselves. Many of us use that "looking-good kid" image so well that others think they know us when they don't. When they realize we don't open up to them, they feel cheated. Maureen didn't even realize she was holding herself back.

Carol and I were best friends, I thought. I went over to her house all the time. People at church teased us about being twins. Whatever project Carol worked on, everyone knew I was close behind.

Carol called me one night and told me about a problem she was having with her husband. I re-

minded her that my husband and I had gone through the same thing and I told her that her faith in God would see her through. She distanced herself from me after that and I was hurt. When we hashed this out, she explained that she felt like I always gave her pat answers instead of showing her my real self. I never admitted my problems to her until they were over. I always seemed to be on top of things. "You're not real and I don't feel comfortable around you," she told me.

How could I tell Carol that I was broken inside most of the time? Why couldn't I trust this friend with my secret anxieties? I never imagined that she wanted that from me. No one else had ever listened to me or wanted to get that close to me. As a kid, I was expected to do the cooking and keep quiet. As an adult, it's always been easier to hold back a little of myself.

Maureen's experience is common. She learned to act as if she were close to Carol, but to stay distant from her. It surprised her that Carol said this, because most people didn't mind that she kept back her true opinions and feelings. Besides Maureen, a placater child, got her kudos in relationships from helping other people. She dropped everything to listen to other people's woes and give advice. "People would think we were close because I helped them," says Maureen, "but all that pseudo-intimacy protected me from opening up about my true fears and doubts."

Fearing abandonment

You don't have to have been left on a hospital doorstep as a baby to feel abandoned. With the Fall in Eden came a sense of abandonment that won't be fulfilled until we get to the other side of heaven. Here on earth, the people we care about have their own problems, and without realizing it, they may abandon us emotionally. When we need someone to hold us, or to talk to us, they aren't available. The more these abandonments occur, however, the deeper is that feeling that we will be forgotten, that no one will come for us when we need them.

If our fears of abandonment are pervasive enough, we may cling to those we love to the point that we suffocate them. Margaret tells her perspective:

I have leaned on everyone I know to solve my problems. I would call people and then call them back. In past dating relationships, I've sucked the life out of guys because I was so afraid they would dump me.

The truth is that I'm afraid everyone will leave me. I can remember my parents talking about divorce all the time. I worried how we would make it if Mom left us. Or would she take us with her? Where would we get money to live on? I replayed these thoughts in my mind and imagined what it would be like if I had to take care of our family. What would I do if I came home and found my mother gone? I did end up losing my relationship with my grandma because my dad said she was the cause of my mom's problems. We didn't see her for five years. Up to that point, she had been the stabilizing influence in our lives.

It has taken me a while to learn how to lean on people without bowling them over. I've had to learn to spend more time with God, to journal about all the fears inside me. I'm learning that relationships are about giving to other people instead of using them to get what I need.

Other times, fears of abandonment cause people to limit the depth of relationships. Craig, for example, keeps his problems to himself. He learned this as a child when he came home to an empty house. When his parents came home, they never talked openly about problems, so he doesn't know how. This tendency to be extremely independent extends even to God. Even though he leads a Bible study, he says, "I don't trust God in my heart of hearts. I hide this distrust and act as if my life is humming along. My spiritual life is at a plateau—I'm numb to spiritual things."

Shedding our alienation requires that we crawl out of our shell and reach out to safe people who will let us talk about our doubts and feelings without condemning us. We may find them within the church, which God created to function as the arms and legs and shoulders of Christ's body. It's true that these people will disappoint us, but that doesn't mean all is lost. The more we learn to trust people here on earth, the more we can trust a God who will never disappoint us and we can stop suspecting that He will fail us.

Tension

The anger and hostility in our culture have let us know that it's wise to keep your guard up. You never know when you'll be accosted on the street. Some of us protect ourselves emotionally by acting as if every event is a potential catastrophe and then being pleasantly delighted if something goes right. The tension shows itself in the following ways.

Working at having fun

Tension can be a pattern for children who sat on the porch and blew bubbles until they heard arguments begin in the house. They may have either listened fearfully from the steps or run to the corner of the yard so they couldn't hear.

Our culture as a whole is now so unskilled at fun that it works at playing. We go to great lengths to find enjoyment. We can't just go to a nearby lake or beach; it isn't fun unless we go to an island resort. Even then, fun somehow doesn't feel right. A fun-filled vacation supposedly means seeing every tree and mud hole in four days.

Or, checking items off in a tour book signals that we've had fun.

Taking ourselves too seriously

Judging ourselves without mercy can lead to being extra sensitive to criticism. Even a little criticism brings us down. Here's an example of how Jan took life too seriously even as a child and now as an adult:

As a fourth grader, I was caught talking with my friend Rhonda when we were supposed to be working. I felt guilty because I liked my teacher so much and wanted to please her.

The teacher corrected us in a winsome way, but I took it hard. Rhonda giggled.

Then the teacher said, "At least Rhonda giggled. Jan just looked at me as if she had seen a horror show." The class laughed, but I didn't.

I was confused. Wasn't it terrible to be caught talking? Why did Rhonda laugh? Wasn't I supposed to act repentant when I was wrong?

Over twenty years later, I still remember how upset and embarrassed I was. I wanted to be light-hearted like Rhonda, but I just couldn't. I see now that the teacher felt sad that I had taken it so hard. She tried to get me to lighten up.

I'm just now learning not to take mistakes so seriously. I marveled at a friend who laughed when she forgot the words as she sang the special music at church. The congregation even laughed with her. A few years ago, I probably would have cried on the platform. Now I could keep going, but cry later. Someday I hope to be able to laugh at myself as she does.

The danger of taking life too seriously is that we begin to view ourselves and our every action as all-important in the universe. In the larger perspective of life, God is in

control, and our mistakes and difficulties aren't so cata-
strophic: "For our light and momentary troubles are
achieving for us an eternal glory that far outweighs them
all. So we fix our eyes not on what is seen, but on what is
unseen. For what is seen is temporary, but what is unseen is eternal" (2 Cor. 4:17-18).

Acting irresponsibly or super-responsibly

When children grow up with distracted adults, they may
not finish homework or extracurricular projects. As they
become adults, they may have difficulty following a
project through from beginning to end or putting them
off until the last moment. Things only work well when
someone stands over them.

Some overreact to their irresponsibility by becoming
super-responsible. They vow they'll change and they go
overboard to prove themselves. The super-responsible
role becomes comfortable because it can be difficult to
trust others to follow through. If both extremes sound
familiar, you're not alone. Many times we bounce back
and forth between them, behaving super-responsibly one
day and irresponsibly the next.

Creating chaos wherever we go

If you've grown up with arguing or confusion, chaos feels
normal. As an adult, you may thrive on chaos and perform well in crises. When things go too well, it feels
wrong. People raised this way often report they don't
date "nice guys" or "nice girls" because they're not exciting enough. They're "hooked on drama" and may create dramatic stories to impress people.

Letting go of the tension means that we rehearse ways
to shut off the panic button in situations that recreate
feelings from the past. We loosen up and lighten up by
opening up to people who understand our tension, who
can even laugh at how tense they are. We cultivate the
playful, hopeful part of ourselves, that doesn't care what

other people think, the part that can become totally absorbed in play and creative pursuits. We let go of the layers of sophisticated "shoulds." By trading our sophistication for simplicity and our "looking-good kid" image for authenticity, we free ourselves to explore and enjoy life. We can relax and let go of our desire for the adrenaline rush of chaos.

You May Be Wondering . . .

Q *What's so wrong with wanting to be in control? Isn't self-control a fruit of the spirit?* (Gal. 5:22-23)

A Self-control is helpful, but when people try to control what is not within their control—whether a hurricane will hit, whether people will like us or not, whether children will make right decisions while away from home—they assume a role that is God's role alone. Often this preoccupation with control disturbs our peace of mind (*What if . . . ?*) or we use it to manipulate others. We work so hard at controlling our environment that we no longer surrender circumstances, people, and problems to God.

Q *If Christians are supposed to count others better than themselves, isn't it OK to feel less adequate?*

A We are commanded to "in humility consider others better than [ourselves]" (Phil. 2:3), but we do so because we follow the example of Jesus Christ who willingly emptied Himself even though He knew He was the Son of God (Phil. 2:6-11). He didn't die on the Cross because He believed He wasn't worth much or that God had better things to do that day. To reflect the truth of this passage, we need to understand our great self-worth in God's eyes—His children for whom He gave His Son, His flock, His priests. From that honored position, we learn to reflect the love of Christ and give up our love for convenience, our love for attention, our love for being served.

Personal Reflection

Choose three or four of these questions and share the answers with a group or friend.

● What kinds of changes or situations are most difficult for you? What part of that situation is within your control? What part is not?

● When is it most difficult to tell the truth? To whom? What is it about this person or situation that makes it hard to tell the truth?

● Do you tend to be more impulsive or more analytical?

● When are you hardest on yourself? Whose approval or affirmation would you most like to have? What is it about that person that makes you want to please him or her?

● Are you more likely to stay distant from people or to want to be perhaps too close too quickly?

● In what ways do people try too hard to have fun?

● Which parts of your life do you take too seriously?

CHAPTER NINE

Numbing the Pain

If we've buried a significant amount of tension and frustration in our holding tank, we've come up with various ways to manage it over the years. Innocent (or not so innocent) behaviors become our "fix," so to speak and we come to depend on them. Here's Tom's story of how he numbed his negative feelings.

When I was a freshman in high school, my parents gave me three pairs of polyester bell-bottom pants. One pair was green, another was brown, and the other was navy blue. They were all too short. When I asked if I could have some Levis, my mom said, "You have the most beautiful pants. Why don't you wear them?"

My mom was a powerful woman and I couldn't make her understand. I felt guilty because I was the minister's son but I wanted to look like my friends at school. I couldn't stand to wear the polyester pants so I wore one of the two pairs of jeans I owned every other day. Then my friends teased me about wearing those pants all the time. Still, it was better than wearing those "flood pants."

About that time, I became obsessed with lust. I couldn't get a hold of pornography so I searched the women's magazines for scantily-clad women. I felt so guilty that I practiced a self-torturing type of masturbation ritual. That didn't ease the guilt or pain. At thirteen, I molested a two year old. My dad talked to a psychologist and told me, "Your sister had a similar incident once." Then he dropped it.

At sixteen, I began practicing bulimia. I would eat three plates of food, throw up and then eat dessert. I ran fifty miles a week. My entire family was overweight and I didn't want to be like them. After ten years of this, I saw that I was destroying my body, so I tried to channel this frenzy into workaholism. I quit throwing up, but I still felt inadequate. I became a respectable family man and church leader hoping to hide my pain in serving others.

As I talked about my depression with my wife, I realized how hurt I was by my childhood. I never realized that I was using all these addictions to numb my feelings and forget my past. In therapy and support groups, I looked at childhood feelings and let go of them. I saw how I had copied my parents' addictions with food and work. My parents have always craved sweets and they could never relax. On holidays, it wasn't unusual for them to have Monopoly tournaments that lasted fifteen hours!

I still attend a support group for sexual addiction and I'm learning to deal with my feelings rather than retreating to lust. Both my career and my marriage are beginning to blossom. I'm learning that I don't have to please other people. I can be me—and people might even like me better for it.

In Tom's search to find things to numb his feelings, he tried sex, food, and work, but they didn't help. Like many Christians, he skipped over the church taboos: alcoholism and drug addiction.

Almost any substance or behavior can become an addiction, including: nicotine, caffeine, religion, relationships, sex, eating, exercising, spending money, gambling, or watching TV. Many compulsions seem innocent. Mom reads romance novels to fill the emptiness in her life. Dad builds furniture or works on the car out in the garage to hide from a family that talks about feelings. Sooner or later, they find themselves trapped in what is called the addictive cycle:

Preoccupation: I think about it; I look forward to it.

Ritualization: I prepare for it by thinking, *This afternoon everyone will be gone and I can have time to . . . or I'll need this (a drug, food, and so on) later when I . . . .*

Compulsive Behavior: I act out the obsession and feel good for a while. That feel-good time shortens, until it lasts for as little as a few seconds.

Guilt: I feel guilty that I acted out. To relieve these bad feelings, I return to preoccupation.

If a parent depended on a substance or behavior, we may imitate that parent's dependency or we may try hard not to use their dependency, only to choose another one. Even though the specific manifestation is different, the drivenness to numb negative feelings is the same.

Drivenness is a powerful, but overlooked force. First Timothy 6:10 describes drivenness well, saying that it isn't money, for example, that is the root of evil, but, *"the love of* money." In the same way, *the love of* food, *the love of* alcohol, *the love of* work, brings forth all kinds of evil behavior. At the root of that drivenness is hurt and anger that the answers to those core questions — *What must I do to feel loved? What must I do to feel valued?* — have disappointed us.

Food
Compulsive eating and dieting

To eat compulsively is to use food and eating as a soothing agent just as alcoholics use alcohol. Compulsive eat-ers give a lot of time and thought to food. They look forward to eating, especially when they're alone. They may eat a salad when they meet a friend for lunch but after they bid the friend good-bye, they load up on ice cream. Some have called compulsive eating the "Christian sin" because with church potluck dinners, fund raising events, and ice cream socials, it's difficult to avoid it.

Since magazines, movies, and TV tell us that to be thin is to be attractive, people feel driven to lose weight. The compulsion to overeat and then to lose weight creates a yo-yo effect, typical of compulsions.[1]

Looking for love in all the wrong places

Eating disorders

Bulimics eat large quantities of food, usually "forbidden foods," and then purge themselves by vomiting, over-exercising, or taking laxatives. Others ease their pain by starving themselves. Anorexics get high from feelings of starvation and control. They usually see themselves as fat no matter how thin they are. Many people assume that only adolescent women are bulimic or anorexic, but this isn't true. Men and women of all ages use these disorders to control weight and feel good about life.

Media

Watching television for hours and reading books in which fantasies come true seems to provide fulfillment when life is too stressful to face.

As Laura's marriage crumbled, she read romance novels non-stop. "What harm does it do? I used to ask," says Laura. "They weren't pornographic. I wasn't watching TV—I was expanding my mind. I could consume a few chapters while I stirred the soup. When Christian friends told me these books were garbage, I said, At least I'm not out sleeping with men like a lot of people I know."

Laura stopped reading romance novels the day she came home and found her husband packing his bags. "The game was over and I had to channel my energy into putting the relationship back together. Life wasn't like those novels. In real life, the hero was leaving the scene and I, the damsel, was sad. There was no romance writer to fix it."

Work

Workaholism is not the love of hard work; it's working compulsively for reasons that have little to do with work. People become hooked on productivity because they need to be needed, they need to control, or they need to feel that they accomplished something to feel worth-while.

Tom's parents were "busyness addicts." His dad was a minister and worked eighty hours a week to be exactly what his congregation wanted. He began promising his wife that he would be home by 9:00 P.M., but he found that time flies when you're using work to feel good about yourself so he didn't make it. Even though he knew he was placing stress on his family, he kept doing it.

Some workaholics are perfectionists too. They can't relax and they can't tolerate failure. They're driven by a desire to be "good enough" and their short-lived victories are their "highs."

Hooked on "Good Things"

When we're needy inside, nearly anything can become a crutch to us, as Kathleen discovered.

After I gave birth to my second child, I slept more than usual because I was so tired. As time passed, I felt distanced from my husband (who's a pastor) and confused by all the ruckus at church. I wanted to get away, so I slept as much as I could. It was so peaceful to sleep—no babies crying, no telephones ringing. I looked forward to naps and got angry if I couldn't have them. I quit praying—I used sleep to forget my worries.

That normal task of owning and acquiring things can become an obsession. We don't shop till we drop, but we find ourselves preoccupied with that next new item on sale, scouring the catalogs for bargains. When Dean tried to cut down his book buying, he found that borrowing a book didn't give him the good feeling that buying books had. He liked owning them, displaying them and looking as if he were "in the know." He felt secure that certain books were on his shelf should he ever need them.

Religious Addiction

All types of faiths have religious addicts, but let's examine how this addiction manifests itself in Christian circles.

Hooked on volunteerism

Churchaholics are involved with church as many days of the week as possible. Outside the church, they lose their niche and their identity. They may even distance themselves from friends, relatives, and spouses who don't overinvolve themselves in church. They've always wanted to be "good enough" and church workaholism has shown them how. In the story below, Charlie describes how he has felt.

> *I feel guilty if I'm not at every church event. I had to skip a leadership meeting to go my son's sixth grade graduation and I felt guilty! I lead a midweek Bible study and I have never asked anyone to fill in for me no matter how sick I've been. I don't want the pastor to think I'm not committed. I don't want someone to ask, "So, where is Charlie?"*

Hyperinvolvement in church activities is especially subtle because it's easy to hide a desire to look good under a sincere desire to serve God. The hyperinvolved are popular, they're loved, they're admired, but at home the family is asking, "Where's my dad? Where's my wife?" How do you argue with someone who's giving his or her life to God? Doing significant things can be a "drug of choice" to feel loved and valued.

Hooked on "highs"

Those seeking religious "highs" look for newer, better, more exciting experiences to help them maintain or recapture intense emotions. To create this fervor, they may spend a lot of time attending church activities, talking about new Bible insights, or watching Christian TV programs. Since religious "highs" satisfy the emotions but not the inner spirit, it takes more and more of this frenzied activity to maintain a "high." Finally, the person crashes.

Hooked on rigidity

Many perfectionistic religious addicts have grown up in strict authoritarian homes where there was no give and take. As children, they wanted to fly a kite or build a fort, but their parents didn't consider that spiritual so it wasn't allowed.

Now as adults, they carry doctrine and practices to extremes. Every area of life becomes good or bad. They feel guilty about engaging in activities they've been taught are wrong, even if they don't believe it now. They maintain a facade of perfection and don't dare admit their fear, guilt, and anger. They refuse to listen to their teenagers' typical "crises of faith" questions such as, "How can I be sure that God exists?"

Hooked on a leader

Have you ever talked with someone who constantly says, "My pastor says . . . ," or who frequently quotes a religious celebrity? Frequently, this is a person who lacks intimate relationships and is looking for someone to fill their needs. Even greater damage occurs if that leader motivates followers by shaming them as second-class Christians and even threats of losing salvation. Followers who remain loyal to a shaming leader often come from an authoritarian family and feel comfortable being told what to do. Those from families with few convictions can become devoted to a leader because they believe they've finally found the strength that was lacking in their parents.

None of this is to say that all Christians who go to church, read their Bibles, and pray several times a day are addicted. Someone has said, "You can never get too much of God," and that is true. The problem is that religious addicts don't seek God; they seek emotional highs, self-righteousness, or extreme forms of control. Christians who are devoted truly to God rely on Him as the author of wholeness and seek a deeper relationship with Him.

Chemical Addiction
Alcohol

Even if someone doesn't get drunk, the dependency on alcohol shows itself in doing whatever it takes not to miss a Friday night in the bar. It becomes a reward for a week's work and a way of numbing the frustration of an empty existence.

Studies have shown that four times as many adult children of alcoholics become substance abusers as those who didn't grow up in alcoholic families.[2] While researchers look for genetic links, the behavioral link is obvious—alcoholic parents set an example of turning to a substance to fill unmet needs.

Drugs

Nicotine, sugar, and caffeine are technically drugs because they alter the structure or function of the body when used. They produce a physical high and low in most people. They become a compulsion when they're used regularly to manage pain, to energize, or to relax. Prescription drugs, designed to alleviate physical pain, can become habit forming when used to mask emotional pain. The "addict" then runs from doctor to doctor in search of one more quick fix. Even illegal drugs are more common in church circles than one might think. Baby boomers who smoked marijuana as hippies in the 60s now wear business suits and relax at home with the same habit. One woman lamented about her husband:

> *I'm trying to get my husband more interested in church. He finally came with me and we met a couple he liked. We had them over and what do you know? He and the other husband smoked marijuana together. The other wife and I were sick. Instead of helping each other, these men were comparing favorite pipes and special blends. I felt so discouraged.*

Sexual Addiction

Numbing out with sexual activity occurs at three levels, according to psychologist Dr. Patrick Carnes.[3]

Level One: masturbation, repeated promiscuous relationships, pornography and strip shows, prostitution, and homosexuality.

Level Two: exhibitionism, voyeurism, indecent calls, and liberties.

Level Three: molestation, incest, rape, sexual violence.

Many sex addicts were sexually abused as children. In their loneliness and alienation, they're reliving those experiences. The good news is that more counselors and literature are dealing with sexual addiction.

Surrendering the Drivenness

Our purpose is to help you examine the ways you're protecting yourself and so this chapter is included to probe your thoughts. Many excellent books and support groups are available on these topics. Not everyone who drinks alcohol is an alcoholic nor is every overweight person a compulsive eater. Here are some questions to help you determine if your behavior is compulsive:

- Does this activity give me a false sense of comfort, pride or power?
- Is this activity harming me in any way? Do I harm others or overlook them because of this activity?
- Does this activity follow the addictive cycle: preoccupation, ritualization, acting out, guilt?

Those who answer yes to these questions may be relying on behavior that is damaging themselves and others. The obvious, but short-sighted solution is to simply stop these behaviors. Some do succeed through steeled self-control, but this route usually forces people to bury pain instead of facing it. It also increases false images of personal strength, which sets them up for more failure.

The better methods for treatment include a combination of relating to others and relating to God such as the processes and tools we'll describe in upcoming chapters. Curbing the outward behavior is never enough; the behavior is being driven by inner pain that must be faced — and healed.

You May Be Wondering . . .

Q *What if my friend, child, or spouse is addicted? What can I do?*

A We can do little for a friend or relative who is addicted until they are desperate enough to do something for themselves. We can, however, work on ourselves and set better boundaries so their addictions do not harm us. By looking at our motives and examining our pasts, we not only set an example they will probably notice, but we also become more compassionate and open. They may become more likely to talk to us as we give up our "fixing" ways and offer glimpses of God's unfailing love.

Q *If I have alcoholic parents, does that mean I'm going to be an alcoholic too?*

A Certain influences are working against you. You have watched your parents manage their pain through drinking, and most of us imitate our parents' behaviors whether we want to or not. Also, studies show that some people have a genetic predisposition to alcoholism meaning that their genes are set up so that they are more likely to crave alcohol. You may be one of them.

Having alcoholic parents doesn't mean you are doomed to become an alcoholic. However, it may mean that your satiation level is higher, that it takes more alcohol to get you drunk, or that you want to drink until you're drunk. This predisposition can act as a caution that drinking alcohol is not a safe activity for you, especially if you're working through emotional pain.

Personal Reflection

Choose three or four of these questions and share the answers with a group or friend.

• It seems as if most people in western culture are dependent on something. What would you say is the most common addiction among your friends or family?

• What do you do to get out of a bad mood? When you feel lonely? When you need to be perked up?

• Take the following self-test and judge if the activity you mentioned in the last question is a compulsion. Does this activity give me false sense of comfort, pride, or power? Is this activity harming me in any way? Do I harm others or overlook them because of this activity? Does this activity follow the addictive cycle: preoccupation, ritualization, acting out, guilt?

• Who can you talk to who also struggles with this behavior?

CHAPTER TEN

Blurred Spiritual Vision

How do you picture God? Have you ever viewed Him as:

- a Santa Claus, who rewards us only if we're good?
- a detached Father Time, who isn't available?
- a cosmic prison guard, who watches every move?
- the Wicked Witch of the West (from *The Wizard of Oz*), who is out to get us?
- a whining grandmother, wringing her hands and telling us to be good?
- a fair-weather friend who abandons us when illness or trouble darkens our lives?

Our culture has long perpetuated the untruth that God loves good people — so be good! From this distorted view, children often conclude that God loves them more if they get A's on tests, clean their room, and brush their teeth. Children look to their parents whom they perceive to be all-powerful people for clues about God. If their parents are sensitive and take time for them, they see God as one who listens and who takes time. If parents are too busy for them, they may assume God is too busy for them too.

Because of these influences of parents and culture, adults often relate to God the same way they react to life — through the darkened lenses of distrust, self-con-

How do you picture God?

THE WAY GOD REALLY IS	THE WAY WE SEE HIM
loving & caring	hateful & unconcerned
good & merciful	mean & unforgiving
steadfast & reliable	unpredictable & untrust-worthy
unconditional grace	conditional approval
present & available	absent when needed
giver of good gifts	takes away good things, "killjoy"
nurturing & affirming	critical & unpleasable
accepting	rejecting
holy, just & fair	unjust, unfair, partial

demnation, alienation, and tension. After years of interacting with God in these ways, it's difficult to believe the
biblical truth that God loves them no matter what, that
He longs to forgive them when they fail Him. David
Seamands points out in his book, *Healing of Memories,*
how the hurts of our past can distort one's view of God
in the following ways.[1]

Most Christians would deny ever viewing God as He's
described in the right column because the Bible says that
God is love. A distortion develops in which we say we
believe God is love even if we don't sense it. The following common phrases reveal a tyrant view of God:

- God must be upset with me now.
- This is fun—it must be sin, right?
- Where is God when you need Him?
- God zapped me into shape today.

The last statement echoes the jokes we make about
God sending lightning bolts on people if they disobey.
Do we speak more truthfully what we believe about God
in jokes than we would ever admit in serious conversa-
tion? Here's how Jan wrestled with this tyrant view of
God.

*Every time something went wrong, I felt as if God
were picking on me, that He was mad at me. It
could be something even as trivial as a stopped-up
drain or misplaced insurance forms, but I would
feel that God was working against me. With each
trial I experienced, I became more hardened
against God. I developed a spiritual chip on my
shoulder, expecting problems at every turn.*

*The worst part of it is that I knew in my mind
that God wasn't like that. I'd taught Bible studies
for years and written dozens of Bible school lessons. I searched the Scripture for passages about
God's love and studied them over and over. I tried
so hard to make my heart believe them, but I kept
responding to God as if he were a punishing, stingy*

tyrant. I could have won an intellectual debate defending God's love, but I still felt deep inside as if He were picking on me.

"Looking Good" Christians

If you grew up in a respectable church family with a King Baby parent, the distortion about God may be even greater. You may have felt that the church approved of the selfish behavior of the King Baby parent, even if they didn't know how extreme it was. This confirmed your worst fears that the church was just like your family: an unsafe place to talk, trust, or feel.

No matter how large or small the distortion, the result is that we act as if God is not someone with whom we can truly talk, trust or feel. When we read the Psalms, we don't recognize how safe David was to show his feelings to God with outlandish statements. When we hear about Moses before the burning bush, we don't see how he felt safe to talk to God, to even offer excuses. When we hear about Joshua asking God to make the sun "stand still," we miss that he trusted God to intervene in this unheard of way on Israel's behalf (Ps. 35; Exod. 3:1-4:17; Josh. 10:12).

This tendency to say one thing, but believe another creates distortions in the way we interpret Scripture. It's as if we're so entrenched in distrust, self-condemnation, alienation, and tension that they create roadblocks in our thinking and a traffic jam occurs between our minds and hearts. Much of our journey of self-examination involves getting the truths about God through that traffic jam and into our hearts.

Distorting Scripture
Being good enough

The Good News becomes Bad News when the Bible is interpreted to mean that Christians have no worth or that they have to work tirelessly to please God. This encourages people to play people-pleasing games with God instead of surrendering themselves to Him. God is willing to carry the burden of our obedience, even our hurts and mistakes: "Come to Me, all you who are weary and burdened, and I will give you rest. Take My yoke upon you and learn from Me, for I am gentle and humble in heart, and you will find rest for your souls. For My yoke is easy and My burden is light" (Matt. 11:28-30).

Sanitizing the saints

Today's Christians would never elect to a church office most of the heroes of the Bible. Paul—a mass murderer? David—a murderer and adulterer? Jacob/Israel—an extortionist who cheated his own brother out of what was rightfully his? Abraham and Isaac—men who offered their wives to be used sexually to save their own lives? These normal human beings who loved God have been cleaned up to the point that we lose sight of how their sinfulness makes them accessible role models for us. Their blatant sin also makes our attempts to be looking good kids appear ridiculous. We have mistakenly believed that the Bible is written about humans becoming good people when it's actually a testimony to God's goodness and grace.

Sanitizing biblical figures adds to that feeling that we have to fake it to be good Christians. In reality, biblical characters were real people and their lives can give hope to the most shadowy parts of ourselves.

"Love thy neighbor"

This verse has been misinterpreted to mean that we should be caretakers, giving into the whims of people who harm us. *Agape* love, however, can be tough as well as patient. In the Old Testament, God loved the nation of Israel even though they worshiped idols and practiced human sacrifice. He gave them many chances to repent through the prophets He sent. Yet God did not allow

Himself to be abused when Israel ignored His warnings. The northern kingdom was scattered forever and the slightly less wicked southern kingdom was taken into captivity and then returned to its homeland.

Loving our neighbor means copying God's ways. He's not only patient and loving, but also firm and discerning: "Each of us should please his neighbor *for his good,* to build him up" (Rom. 15:2) [emphasis ours]. It doesn't do a King Baby parent, friend, or spouse any good to allow them to continually speak hurtfully to us. We love each other and build each other up by "speaking the truth in love" (Eph. 4:15). "I love you, Dad, but I will not allow you to speak to me that way."

Instant joy and peace

For those who tend to be tense or depressed, the following verses are ripe for misinterpretation:

Rejoice in the Lord always. I will say it again: Rejoice! . . . Do not be anxious about anything but in everything, by prayer and petition, with thanksgiving, present your requests to God. And the peace of God, which transcends all understanding, will guard your hearts and your minds in Christ Jesus. Finally brothers, whatever is true, whatever is noble, whatever is right, whatever is pure, whatever is lovely, whatever is admirable — anything that is excellent or praiseworthy — think about such things (Phil. 4:4, 6-8).

Curt latched onto these verses as a quick ticket to happiness, but then resented them because they seemed so impossible.

I never felt like rejoicing. It's hard to rejoice when you haven't seen it modeled in your family. I wondered if there were a secret to this rejoicing. Maybe if I performed the right ritual the right way, I could rejoice and have peace.

When I began having problems in life, it got worse. I felt that the phrase, "think about these [positive] things," meant that if I shut out the pain of my past and ignored my upbringing, I would be OK. I had already tried that—it's called denial—and it hadn't worked. It reminded me of a parent who spanks you unjustly and then says, "Now smile." I knew that facing my pain was helping me get better. Why was the Bible saying otherwise? Why was "the peace that passes all understanding" passing me by?

Joy and peace are time-release capsules, not instant uppers. Rejoicing in the Lord isn't the same as "being up." It can occur in the midst of pain, just as Paul wrote these words from prison. We learn that by loving God and focusing on Him we can praise Him even when everything else looks hopeless. One powerful way to focus on "whatever is true" (Phil. 4:8) is to face past hurts so we can go on to focus on positive things "that are lovely."

Legalistic formulas

As masters of self-condemnation, we use Bible verses to beat ourselves over the head. Jan used to feel guilty when she read the above passage in Philippians.

"Rejoicing in the Lord" was an achievement far beyond me. This was "advanced Christianity" reserved for special people, which meant that I was a second-class Christian. I felt hopeless. Depression had hovered over me my entire life and I didn't think I could ever rejoice in the Lord always.

I was so desperate for peace that I turned verses 6-7 into a spiritual formula:

Step 1—work hard at rejoicing; Step 2—pray; Step 3—wait for peace to land in my lap. It was similar to using a facial—spread it on, let it dry for ten minutes, wash it off, and you have perfect skin. It sounds silly that I did that, but it seemed normal for me since I'd already read dozens of quick-fix, multi-step, self-help books.

As I learned ways to ventilate my hurt and anger, that daily depression lifted. I still don't rejoice in the Lord always, but I've tasted it. God's joy and peace creep up on me more and more and replace the inner chaos. From talking with more mature Christians, I see that rejoicing in the Lord is tough even for them. Again, I was judging myself without mercy.

I've quit using Scripture as a spiritual hickory switch to beat myself. It's much easier to grow in God, to rest in His peace when I'm not clamoring so much for it. I'm trusting God to work in my life instead of feeling driven to achieve what some people would call, "spiritual success."

Any passage can become a legalistic formula for those who are needy enough. Many act as if some phrases are nearly magic, especially, "Thy will be done" or "in Jesus' name." Supposedly, if you tack those phrases on the end of a prayer, God will automatically grant that request. Instead, those phrases refer to a growing relationship with God in which Christians know Him, seek Him and listen to Him. They have some sense of His will and are eager to avoid acting in any way that is not consistent with Jesus' name and demeanor.

Instant righteousness

Another scriptural idea that may confuse us is being "a new creation" in Christ. Second Corinthians 5:17 says: "Therefore, if anyone is in Christ, he is a new creation; the old has gone, the new has come!" Well-meaning Christians suggest that this Scripture means that we are released from our sin nature, from the past influence of our culture and from everything that has happened in the past.

Becoming a new creation (some versions say "new creature") in Christ isn't an instant process. This lengthy process is described in John 8:32: "Then you will know the truth, and the truth will set you free." Bible teacher Dr. Lawrence Richards says about this passage: "To 'know' the truth is not to intellectually comprehend, but to experience. To know the 'truth' is not to focus on a body of knowledge, but to live in touch with reality as God knows reality."[2]

This experience of living in the reality of God is something in which we grow as we build our relationship with Him. One small part of that includes breaking out of denial and admitting how our past has affected us. As we grow in our understanding that God loves us and transforms us, the more free we are to become "new creatures in Christ."

Violated promises

Have you ever eyed with suspicion those verses that promise God's protection? Perhaps you question verses such as these: "For He will command His angels concerning you to guard you in all your ways; they will lift you up in their hands, so that you will not strike your foot against a stone" (Ps. 91:11-12). Some have wondered, *If this verse were true, an adult who was abused as a child might ask, "Where were those angels when I needed them? Why was my childhood so filled with fear?"*

These verses tell us that God provides angelic protection at certain times. They don't promise that Christians will never have problems or will never suffer unfairly (which is what we often want them to say). If these verses did promise complete protection, no believer would ever have stubbed a toe on a stone! Not only is this conclusion ridiculous, but we know that many of the early Christians were persecuted (Acts 8:1-3) and at least one apostle, James, was beheaded (Acts 12:2).

Part of our problem with verses such as Psalm 91:11-12 is that we want to know why God does what He does. This is part of the human struggle to understand God and His choices, which is not a recommended or practical goal. " 'For My thoughts are not your thoughts, neither are your ways My ways,' declares the Lord. 'As the heavens are higher than the earth, so are My ways higher than your ways and My thoughts than your thoughts' " (Isa. 55:8-9). God knows all, we don't, and we'll become frustrated trying (Isa. 40:13). Instead, our goal is to accept God, seek to know Him and love Him. That limited knowledge is what we call faith. As we do so, we find peace even with things we don't understand. We may still question God at times, as the Psalmist certainly did, but we do so to know and love Him.

When it looks as if God has violated a promise to us, it's wise to examine the thrust of the Bible passage. Are we searching for what the text actually says or are we putting promises in God's mouth that we desperately want for Him to fulfill? Are we making God in our image?

The above examples of easily misinterpreted Scripture show how we funnel our theology through our life experiences. As we become clearer about how we have viewed life through a smoked glass, we can wipe it clean and reexamine the intent of Scripture. We understand each verse in the context of other biblical passages and quit beating ourselves up with isolated proof-texts.

When we understand Scripture more clearly, it relieves some of our struggle. We may have tried to obey all the commands we've heard from pulpits because we wanted to give our all to God. Yet our feelings were so far removed from those ideas that obedience seemed impos-sible.

We finally understand and accept more of reality as God knows reality:

- God loves us and declares us "good enough"
- His love for us isn't based on our perfect obedience or adherence to the standards of cultural Christianity

- He equips us to love others in healthy ways
- He knows our thoughts — even the evil ones — and works within us to grow
- He keeps every promise, even when we don't understand how He's keeping it.

With this understanding, it's easier to get out of God's way and cooperate with Him as He helps us grow.

You May Be Wondering . . .

Q *Where can I find correct images of God?*
A Meditate and ponder passages in the Bible that picture God's love. Parables are helpful because stories can weave their way through that mind-to-heart traffic jam when facts can't. They help us "know" the truth by experiencing it vicariously through the lives of characters described by Jesus. Here are a few parables that stress God's love:

- the persistent owner of the vineyard (Matt. 21:33-41);
- the shepherd in the Parable of the Lost Sheep who risked everything to find that one lost lamb (Luke 15:3-7);
- the prodigal son's father who must have watched diligently to have seen his son a long way off; like that father, God fully blesses us when we come to Him (Luke 15:20, 22).

Q *I talk to God, yet I still don't feel close to Him. What can I do about that?*
A When we feel starved for love, we may try to use God to get the good feelings we crave. It helps if we switch the goals. Our goal is union with God, knowing Him and coming into relationship with Him, not a bath of good, loving feelings. If we pursue that goal of knowing God and doing His will, the feelings we want so much will more likely come. It's also wise to consider that we can sense God's nearness, but not necessarily feel tingly inside.

Personal Reflection

Choose three or four of these questions and share the answers with a group or friend.

● What, if any, Bible passages or phrases have become formulas for you? If you can't think of any, ask God to show you in the next few days any passages you view in a rigid, legalistic way.

● How do you respond to this verse? "How great is the love the Father has lavished on us, that we should be called the children of God!" (1 John 3:1)

● What quality(ies) on the right side of the following chart describe the way you see God at times? What happened to make you feel that way?

THE WAY GOD REALLY IS	THE WAY WE SEE HIM
loving & caring	hateful & unconcerned
good & merciful	mean & unforgiving
steadfast & reliable	unpredictable & untrust-worthy
unconditional grace	conditional approval
present & available	absent when needed
giver of good gifts	takes away good things, "killjoy"
nurturing & affirming	critical & unpleasable
accepting	rejecting
holy, just & fair	unjust, unfair, partial

● Circle the quality on the left side of the chart that describes an aspect of God you need to absorb more deeply.

● God's "unfailing love" (NIV) or "steadfast love" (KJV) is mentioned over thirty-two times in the Bible (twenty-six times in the Psalms alone). Read five or ten Psalms a day for the next few days, underlining these key words and meditating on these passages.

PART III
Paths for Healing the Hurts

CHAPTER ELEVEN

The Examined Life

I start out the week with the best of intentions, determined to be a contented, obedient Christian. Then something seems to poison my activities and relationships—I try to shake it but it feels as if I can't. It's as if I have a real self (who knows how I really feel) and a church self (who tries to feel how I think I ought to feel) and these two selves compete with each other. I act happy while the real self screams inside.

—an entry from Jan's journal

If you've spent any amount of time acting happy when you feel miserable, you understand what it means to have a real self and a church self. Perhaps you've ignored your real self so much that it doesn't seem to exist anymore. To be genuine with God and others, we have to get reacquainted with the real self.

Living Consciously

When the real self is buried long enough, people forget how to live life consciously. Instead, they live on automatic pilot, not even thinking about their words or actions. They live their lives as victims, reacting to events

137

out of a need for self-protection. They interact with people based on their old family roles (Responsible child, Acting Out child, Adjuster, Placater) rather than seeking God's will and wisdom in a situation.

When people set aside their true thoughts and feelings, they often imitate others who seem to know what they think and feel—celebrities, church leaders, friends. While parroting what they've been told, they may believe the opposite at the deepest levels. They may tell neighbors that the church is a warm place where they're valued, but at times they believe that no one at church knows, much less values, them at all. They repeat the truth that God loves them, but at times they believe that God doesn't care. They don't think issues through because they're used to letting others do their thinking for them. They may even be afraid to explore what they believe.

When you've lived this way long enough, you present different selves to different people based on what the moment requires. You figure that when people ask, "How are you?" they want you to say you're fine, so you say it. If you told them you were miserable, they would be shocked. In prayers, you may even imitate words and deeds you consider to be Christian, rather than bringing your true thoughts and feelings to God and asking Him to work with you. After a while, life lacks authenticity.

If we follow a continuous routine of not thinking, trusting or feeling, we shut out the people we love and numb our relationship with God. Because we don't truly connect with people, we may not feel guilty about using them, especially if they use us. People we love may have no idea of how we really feel because we try to make as few waves as possible. It may even result in living life barely conscious: staying with a job we hate; giving in to others' demands; going to church but tuning out. Pam found herself living this way.

I dated a man for four years in college. Everyone assumed we would get married—except me. I couldn't be honest with him and tell him that he was not the man I wanted to marry. I'd figured it out after a few months of dating, but I just couldn't tell him. All those years in college, I told him what he wanted to hear—that he was a great guy and we would go here and there in the future. I never said I'd marry him, but I never said I wouldn't.

I let this go on until graduation when he pressed me about when we would get married. I couldn't face myself. I didn't mean to hurt him. I didn't mean to lead him on, but I had. I explained it to him the best I could in a letter. Writing it out that day I could see that I had lived my life making decisions I regretted, promises I couldn't deliver, and choices to avoid pain.

Months of prayer and talking and self-examination led me to look at my past. My father had left my mother and sisters so many times. I was afraid that if I made a commitment, that would happen to me. I never wanted to be left, to be alone like my mother was. I was living my life trapped in my mother's life. Even if I had understood this, I never could have explained it to my boyfriend. I'm an adjuster; I don't make waves. Because I lived without thinking, I hurt this man I treasured.

To go off automatic pilot and live consciously sounds like too much work. We would have to examine our lives, motives, beliefs and actions. We would have to shake the doubts that say: *I'm just this way. I can't behave any other way.* We would have to stop being victims of our past and believe God can give us a better future.

By God's grace, we can choose to do the work to live authentically, to live with the intention of finding union with God and letting Him transform us into His likeness. We can admit that we are still little children inside— trying to find love, approval and value. We can grieve that our pretending has harmed ourselves and others and sidetracked God's purposes for us.

To live consciously, we have to listen to ourselves, weigh what we hear in light of God's work in our life and act on that reflection. Then we find out what it means to be engaged in life, making the most of this moment, not focused on yesterday or tomorrow.

The Examined Life

To live in the truth, we must be willing to undergo rigorous self-examination, saying, "Test me, O LORD, and try me, examine my heart and my mind" (Ps. 26:2). We also examine how we relate to others, especially those in the body of Christ (1 Cor. 11:28-29). Viewing ourselves with God's infinite grace, we become aware of our motives and ask ourselves these questions:

- How do I *feel?*
- What do I *think?*
- What will I *do?*

How Do I Feel?

If you've lived on automatic pilot for years, this can be a difficult question to answer. You may not be used to noticing feelings and have no idea what the feeling is. Or you may have lived under the *should* of being "inright, outright, upright, downright happy all the time" and feel you've fallen so far short of that goal that you don't want to know how you feel. If you've numbed your feelings for years, you may want to ask God to unearth your feelings for you and help you identify them. Here's a list of common feelings to help you identify what's going on inside you.

aggressive	anxious	apologetic
arrogant	bashful	bored
cautious	confident	confused
determined	disappointed	disapproving

disbelieving	disgusted	ecstatic
enraged	envious	exasperated
exhausted	frightened	frustrated
grieved	guilty	happy
horrified	hurt	indifferent
jealous	lonely	mischievous
miserable	obstinate	optimistic
pained	relieved	sad
shocked	stupid	thoughtful
withdrawn		

As soon as we identify the feeling (especially one such as sadness, anger, greed or hatred), we may be tempted to think, *Don't feel that way!* We need to give ourselves some tender mercy and sit with our feelings for a few minutes. This isn't the time to analyze them, just acknowledge them. It's as if we have to lock the door against denial, which may sound like this:

I did a stupid thing. Cross that out. My mom told me not to say anyone is stupid, so I shouldn't be thinking this. But this is how I feel!

I feel stubborn and rebellious, as if I could kick that guy in the teeth. Those aren't very Christian feelings, but that's how I feel.

I feel jealous of her. I shouldn't feel jealous of her, and I know it's silly, but it's true. I'm going to sit here in my jealousy and admit it to myself.

When unearthing feelings, it helps to use various tools such as journaling, talking to a friend or praying about it in a private place. In these safe settings, we can speak out loud and say whatever we feel, and answer ourselves back as the thoughts above illustrate. (Chapter 15 describes these tools in detail.)

What Do I Think?

Once we know the feeling, we step back and look at the reason for the feeling and what it has to do with our behavior. Am I mad because of what someone said to me on the telephone earlier today? Am I feeling obstinate because I want to be right all the time? Am I feeling bashful because I'm withdrawing from the others at work, which is part of my adjuster family role?

After we've sat in our feelings and connected them with our behavior, we can ask that question our culture rushes to first: *How does this feeling square with reality?* It helps to replay the event in our minds to see if we're remembering what happened accurately or if we've slanted it. We tend to distort events—even ones that happened a second ago. For example, if I'm a person who thinks that everyone who squints at me is angry with me, I may have jumped to the conclusion that someone is angry with me.

As we replay the event, we might ask, *Was my reaction appropriate? Did I do something to evoke a reaction from this person? Was I playing an old family role? How does this fit with what I tend to do, based on my history? Is it based on any misconceptions or character defects—laziness, grouchiness, self-centeredness?* It helps to ask these questions with a trusted friend or group because thinking out loud helps us get our perspective straight. A friend may be able to say, Yes, the person seemed angry with you, but he or she may have reacted to you and the way you handled the situation.

Knowing whether our feelings square with reality can be confusing. One of the simplest tools for sorting things out is the serenity prayer: *God, grant me the serenity to accept the things I cannot change, the courage to change the things I can and the wisdom to know the difference.* [1] This prayer shows us that there are two categories of people and situations:

- those I can control to some extent
- those over which I have little or no control.

The second category is by far the larger of the two because we have little control over much in the world. Instead of agonizing over people and circumstances we can't control, we can surrender them and our desire to control them to God. Regarding those things over which we do have control, we do the best we can one day at a time.

What Will I Do?

What does the truth demand that you do to follow through? Sometimes we have to ask for more information. For example, if you're not sure if you misread someone you might want to say, "I'm not sure I understand what just happened. Are you angry with me?"

Once you have enough information, you can consider what options are available. Should you apologize? Or, will apologizing make things worse, and so you should be more careful? How will you respond differently next time? How can you act outside your family role or character defect?

In the beginning, this process can be difficult because our automatic reaction to any dilemma in life is to protect ourselves by *denying* feelings, *blaming* someone else, *isolating* from others, or *acting out in anger* (either in obvious outbursts or hidden manipulation). The more we experience God's grace, however, the more honest we can be with God, even admitting to God such things as:

- I lied because I was afraid people wouldn't like me if they knew the truth.
- I exaggerated today about how many laps I ran because I want people to look up to me.
- I bought that new shirt today to look good because I feel so inadequate compared to the guy I work with. The truth is that he reminds me of my brother who always took advantage of me and so I compete with him.

The more often we speak honestly to ourselves, the easier it gets. For example, when Glenda pulled on the freeway, cutting off someone else, she thought, *I'm turning into a crazy lady—what's going on?* She asked herself the three questions.

How do I feel?

Angry! It's hard for me to admit anger because my sisters don't show their anger. But I'm seething! I need to express this anger, but I'm in a car alone so I can't talk to anyone about this. I'm going to talk to God (even though passers by will think I'm crazy), but I won't release my anger anymore in the way I drive.

What do I think?

I began feeling angry when I left work. What happened there? Could it be that I'm angry because my boss ignored me even though I did such a great job on the project? I thought this wasn't bothering me, but based on the way I'm driving, I'm angry about something and I think that's it.

Is this a pattern for me? *Yes. I frequently get angry when people ignore me—especially men. Why do I do that? I used to feel angry when my father ignored me. Now I manipulate men to get the attention or approval I missed.*

How does this square with reality? *My dad did ignore me, it's true, but I understand now that he had his own problems. He ran two businesses, his political campaigns and his radio show. Maybe he was proving to himself that he was better than his father. I have talked to him about his childhood and mine and I see that he loved me as much as he was able.*

I don't know what he thinks of me now. Come to think of it, though, he tells his friends about my job and how well I'm doing. My hunger for my father to notice me may explain my insatiable need to be noticed. I often do things that embarrass myself just to get attention.

What will I do?

I need to talk to someone about this. I'm going to call my friend who struggles with her feelings about her father. I'm going to admit my unquenchable need to be noticed. (That won't be a proud moment!) I'll ask her to pray that God helps me find a way to understand that I am loved and noticed by Him. I'll see what she's doing about this.

Does this sound complicated? Once we are used to listening to our real selves, it's not as complicated as it may sound. With practice and God's help, it becomes automatic. Glenda's thought processes took only a few minutes. That's a small price to pay for being able to respond to people in authentic, appropriate ways, to do so without exploding, to see God's will for us finally accomplished in our character.

But this is so depressing, some will say. *Who wants to see all these things about yourself that are so negative? This is like a test, and I hate tests!* True, this kind of self-examination described here is a test, but passing or failing isn't the issue. In reality, we all fail every test like this one: "All have sinned and fall short of the glory of God" (Rom. 3:23). So there's no worry about getting good grades or passing the exam. This is more like a diagnostic test. Our goal is simply to see ourselves more clearly. Then we can surrender the results to the only one who has the power to transform us. In that surrender, we ask God to show us what He wants us to do to work through this. Glenda, for example, believed she needed to talk to a friend about it. No matter how badly we feel we fail the test, the result is good: God who loves us helps us to see ourselves more clearly.

As our listening skills improve, we may find that we've ignored helpful messages our real self has sent us because we've assumed that they were selfish or lazy. As Kerry listened to herself, she discovered all kinds of motives.

I was supposed to go to a committee meeting, but I had this feeling that I didn't want to go. My dutiful conscience (well trained as the responsible child of the family) told me, Go anyway. You're one of those people who always shows up. You're not one of those lazy people.

Then I listened to the supposedly lazy feeling for a minute, which said, Those meetings aren't helping anybody!

I asked myself if this were true. Was it an unfruitful meeting? Have I, rescuer that I am, sold myself to a lost cause? *I thought about the meetings and decided they did some good.*

But still, I felt reluctant to go. Was I being lazy? No, I was tired. I was exhausted and needed rest. I knew this was a possibility because I tend to ignore my body's need for rest. So I decided to come home from work early and rest before the meeting.

That helped a lot, but as I got ready to go to the meeting, I still felt reluctant. The face of the committee chairperson flashed in my mind. That was it. I had been irritated with her at a meeting or two, but I had buried it. I snapped at her in the same rebellious way I still snap at my perfectionistic mother. How long am I going to let myself be ruled by my reactions to my parents?

I called a friend and we talked a few minutes about the chairperson's style. We talked about how I could respond firmly, but gently when she made demands on me. I felt a lot better because I was doing the right thing by going to the meeting but I was also paying attention to my thoughts and feelings. As I drove to the meeting, I even prayed for the chairperson!

Daily Process

Strong feelings are only one setting in which this self-examination occurs. At the end of the day, we may want to reflect on the way we interacted with others. We can also ask God to show us our progress: *When today was I serene when I used to be stressed? When today did I forget my normal self-obsession and listen to someone, genuinely absorbing someone else's words?*

We don't view this process as God raking us over the coals, but as gentle steps in the way He transforms us. We understand God to be like the father in the prodigal son story who waited for years for his son to return—not so he could berate the son, but so he could run down the road and greet the repentant boy (Luke 15:20). Every time we uncover an unpleasant truth about ourselves, we receive this awareness with thanks and fall into the Father's arms. We can gently surrender it as God works within us. As we pay attention to ourselves this way, we live more authentically before God and others.

You May Be Wondering . . .

Q *Isn't this kind of self-examination terribly unpleassant?*

A The idea of self-examination is distasteful to some Christians because at times Scripture verses about examination have been misinterpreted to mean that Christians should constantly beat themselves up for their sins. In truth, self-examination doesn't always have to hurt. We can be gentle with ourselves, knowing that God knows our faults better than we do, and still chooses to love us desperately. That's why self-examination and confession are gateways to grace and mercy. God already knows our motives and actions and loves us unconditionally. "There is now no condemnation for those who are in Christ Jesus" (Rom. 8:1) was penned by the apostle Paul, a former mass murderer of Christians. Examining ourselves, then, is a time to see ourselves through God's eyes with His grace and allow Him to open the floodgates of love so that His healing can wash over our wounds.

Personal Reflection

Choose three or four of these questions and share the answers with a group or friend.

● If you chose to live your life on automatic pilot, where would you be twenty years from now?

● Have you gone through a time of rigorous self-examination before? What was it like?

● Think of a recent experience that confused you and work through these questions:

● What do I feel? Anxious? Disgusted? Hopeful? Other?

● What do I think?

● Why do I feel this way? (Based on old roles, misconceptions?)

● How do these feelings square with reality? (Replay the event in your mind.)

● What safe person or place can I find to examine this event with?

● What can I do? (List your options.)

CHAPTER TWELVE

Listening to Ourselves

As we become skilled at examining ourselves, we become more sensitive to our inner thoughts. We may hear cries of anguish and anger that have been stifled for a long time. We have a choice—we can block them, or we can listen to them in the peace of God's presence.

Cries Within

Our deepest thoughts may sound silly and egocentric at times, but they're no more outlandish than the anguished cries of the Psalmists. Sometimes their cries made sense; other times they did not. Sometimes, they were beautiful and poetic; other times, they were full of revenge and self-pity. Whereas we hide our deepest cries in embarrassment, the Psalmists addressed those cries to God. The Jews saw fit to include these extremely emotional and sometimes harsh Psalms in their worship hymnal, a fact that baffles many Christians today.

Some of our cries from within are childlike, reflecting the humility and openness of children that Jesus advised us to seek: "Unless you change and become like little children, you will never enter the kingdom of heaven. Therefore, whoever humbles himself like this child is the greatest in the kingdom of heaven" (Matt. 18:3-4). Ironically, Jesus spoke these words to the disciples as they were behaving childishly—arguing about who would be greatest in the kingdom of heaven. As they indulged their inner cries for fame *(What must I do to feel valued? To be noticed?)*, Jesus urged them to honor the childlike attitudes of humility, simplicity, and trust.

One reason we may have a difficult time hearing the true cries within ourselves and admitting them is that we have picked up so many "shoulds" and have become layered with so much spiritual sophistication. When we become childlike enough to be trustful, innocent, and sold out to a parent who believes in us, we can be honest enough to ask God to help us feel loved. Perhaps you identify with these cries of the psalmists and prophets.

PLEASE TAKE CARE OF ME! PLEASE PROTECT ME! PLEASE PROVE TO ME THAT YOU LOVE ME!

In my distress I called to the LORD;
  I cried to my God for help.
From His temple He heard my voice;
  my cry came before Him, into His ears. . . .
He reached down from on high and took hold of me;
  He drew me out of deep waters.
He rescued me from my powerful enemy,
  from my foes, who were too strong for me. . . .
He brought me out into a spacious place;
  He rescued me because He delighted in me.
                                        Psalm 18:6, 16-17, 19

PLEASE HAVE FUN WITH ME. PLEASE ENJOY ME! PLEASE DELIGHT IN ME! God comes to us as a tender parent, rocking a child:

The LORD *your God is with you,*
  He is mighty to save.
He will take great delight in you,
  He will quiet you with His love,
  He will rejoice over you with singing.
                                        Zephaniah 3:17

PLEASE WIPE MY TEARS.

My eyes fail from weeping,
  I am in torment within, . . .
My eyes will flow unceasingly, without relief,
  until the LORD looks down
  from heaven and sees. . . .
  pour out your heart like water
  in the presence of the Lord.
                              Lamentations 2:11; 3:49-50

PLEASE DO SOMETHING SPECIAL TO PICK ME OUT
AND SHOW ME HOW IMPORTANT I AM TO YOU.

You prepare a table before me
  in the presence of my enemies.
You anoint my head with oil;
  my cup overflows.
Surely goodness and love will follow me
  all the days of my life,
and I will dwell in the house of the LORD forever.
                              Psalm 23:5-6

SOMETHING IS WRONG HERE AND SOMEONE SHOULD
DO SOMETHING ABOUT IT!

Awake, O Lord! Why do You sleep?
Rouse Yourself! Do not reject us forever. . . .
We are brought down to the dust;
  our bodies cling to the ground.
Rise up and help us;
  redeem us because of Your unfailing love.
                              Psalm 44:23, 25-26

When we are free to express these anguished cries to
God in the heat of our self-examination, we gain a greater sense of God's unfailing love for us. The verses we've
heard become more of a reality: "I have loved you with
an everlasting love; I have drawn you with loving-kind-
ness" (Jer. 31:3).

Although God may use other people to help meet our need for love, part of what it means to follow Jesus is to develop a relationship with Him in which we look to Him to meet these needs. An overlooked task of our spiritual journey is to use the necessary tools to understand that:

- God loves us, even when we feel unloved;
- God does all that is necessary to take care of us, even when a loved one dies or we're laid off;
- God enjoys being with us;
- God picks us out by blessing us in unique ways that show how much He longs to satisfy our needs and wants.

Childish Cries

While God as our Father encourages us to come to Him with our childlike cries, our childish cries demand attention too. If we are honest with ourselves, these cries may be self-centered. At times, we care about our needs and not about the goals God has in mind.

Some of our real feelings sound childish because they reflect the impatience of children who never learned delayed gratification. We want what we want when we want it. Maybe we picked this up from our culture that is impatient with failure or from a parent who demanded more: "Make your bed again and do it right this time!" Now as adults, we are horrified to feel these King Baby attitudes erupt within ourselves. We try to cover them up with the church self and pretend to be a looking-good kid who behaves with all the perfection and respectability of a Pharisee. We may keep King Baby safely under wrap until suddenly a particularly painful issue arises at work or at a church board meeting and then we explode. Other people look surprised and wonder what happened.

The King Baby part of us is in operation when our deeper cries resemble these.

I'll do anything to get people to love me

The childish part of the real self will lose seventy pounds to snag a spouse and then gain it back without thinking of how dishonest this is. We may exaggerate, lie, or resort to plastic surgery to obtain the admiration of others.

I'll do anything to get people to notice me

It may be obvious actions such as dressing in conspicuous ways and making brash comments or more subtle ones such as making a joke whenever we're in front of the congregation at church.

I'll do anything to get someone to take care of me

If illness and physical problems have become a way to get others to take care of us, we may search for a doctor who will render a diagnosis that sounds traumatic enough.

I'll squeeze all the fun out of any situation

Parties and fun-loving friends aren't considered celebratory gifts from God, but objects to be manipulated for an escape from reality. If we're in deep pain, we may tell jokes that ridicule others because we'll do whatever it takes to feel as if we're having fun.

When we behave this way, we're using other people to get what we want and they become our victims. It's as if we have a bottomless pit of needs that weren't met as children or from a spouse who left us. So now we feel entitled to take whatever we can get to get our need for love and attention met.

Because these cries sound so selfish, we repress them. But when the holding tank becomes too full, it leaks and we become passive-aggressive, meaning that we find unrelated ways to express our frustration. For example, a husband who is tired of his wife's criticism may make them late for every activity because he knows it gets her in an uproar. Neither of them suspect that his tardiness is simply his anger gone underground.

Sometimes our thoughts imitate a King Baby parent — only many times more harsh. We may scold ourselves, calling ourselves names, "You idiot," or shaming ourselves, "You're worse than. . . ."

If someone could record us saying these things to ourselves, we would be horrified at the harshness in our voice. Sara, who was physically and sexually abused as a child, would often hit herself and yell, No! No! No! She was so used to this kind of treatment that she inflicted it on herself.

As we begin listening to our real selves, it's important not to indulge our King Baby tendencies: "Do not use your freedom to indulge the sinful nature" (Gal. 5:13a). Instead, we become wise nurturing parents to that King Baby part of us that struggles with a me-first mentality. We examine our motives: *Do I have to be right all the time? Do I have to get my way? Am I being manipulative?*

We listen to ourselves patiently, imitating the Son who put children on His lap and listened to them tell their stories. We talk to Him, trust Him, and tell Him what we really feel.

You May Be Wondering . . .

Q *Isn't it self-centered to focus so much on me, myself, and I?*

A If we don't look at ourselves, we'll be victims of our past without realizing it. Just as we have to dig out the weeds to keep them from choking the plants, God empties the pain to let the healing come in.

Perhaps some would try to turn this journey into a self-obsessed fixation on their own needs, but it becomes a self-emptying process for those who use it to seek God. In the rich silence, we see ourselves for who we really are and we hear the motives that drive us. We hear the competing voices, the conflicting motives, the deafening whisper: *Do whatever it takes to feel loved; Do whatever it takes to get attention.*

The primary question in this journey is not, "What about my needs?" but "What is within me and how does God want to shape that?" This process would be self-centered if its goal were to glorify ourselves, that is, to become people who appear cool and confident so that others look up to them. Many times those who pursue becoming a "better me" do so to protect themselves from future pain. For the Christian, becoming a better me or protecting ourselves is not the goal. Our goal is to seek God and find union with Him. Then we're able to show and communicate by word and deed the fruits of the Spirit.

Q *How similar is this idea of listening to our inner cries of anguish to the concepts of "inner child" or "child within"?*

A It's similar in the sense that God encourages us to look within at our motives. He even calls us His children, and we are, because we yearn for completion and we find it in God, our Father.

The term, "inner child," did not originate with the New Age movement, but has been used by psychologists since the 1930s, especially Dr. Hugh Missildine.[1] It usually refers to the intellect and emotions. As Christians, we believe the inner person includes our spirit too because it affects the way we view God. The New Age community uses many psychological and spiritual terms, but that does not taint the words themselves. If the term is helpful, you may wish to use it.

Personal Reflection

Choose three or four of these questions and share the answers with a group or friend.

- Do any of the following deeper cries ring a bell for you? If so, check them.

□ *Please take care of me! Please protect me! Please prove to me that you love me!*

□ *Please have fun with me. Please enjoy me! Please delight in me!*

□ *Please wipe my tears.*

□ *Please do something special to pick me out and show me how important I am to you.*

□ *Something is wrong here and someone should do something about it.*

● If you checked any of these, go back and pray the appropriate Psalm mentioned in this chapter. Write out the response you sense God giving you when you pray this Psalm.

● With which of the following cries do you identify most?

I'll do anything to get people to love me.
I'll trick people into taking care of me.
I'll squeeze all the fun out of any situation.
I'll do anything to get people to notice me.

● What other cries do you see in yourself and the people around you when they're behaving like a King Baby?

● How do any of the passages printed in this chapter answer that inner cry? (If none do, ask God to bring a passage to your attention that does.)

CHAPTER THIRTEEN

We Need Other People

Listening to inner cries and identifying them boldly as we described in the last chapter can be difficult. One of the greatest helps in this is listening to others who are trying to be aware of their own inner motives. Many times they put into words the inner cries we have heard within ourselves but have not named because we lacked the clarity or courage to explore them.

That's why if you stopped reading this book at this point and did not do anything else with the concepts and insights we've presented, you would probably change very little. Why? We need other people not only to help us see ourselves, but also to find healing. If our struggles have come in relationships, so will our healing. Healing comes through finding community, which can be defined as any place where we attach with other people in common purpose. In community, we practice new behaviors and change the way we relate to others. We develop relationships that do reflect God's love and grace—ones in which we feel free to talk, to trust, to feel.

The idea that healing requires community may sound strange because many people believe that knowing a fact enables a person to change behavior. Simply hearing a new insight does not transform the person's ability to obey God because the human spirit is not like a computer that can be reprogrammed. The truth is that we are more than our brains—we are feelings, desires, spirit, body. We can't think ourselves into being better Christians. We can't simply read about a principle of righteousness and then act upon it. On the contrary, a simple reading of the facts can produce a paralyzing guilt. We need to meditate on them and absorb them into our hearts. We need a safe place to reflect on these facts and how they affect every part of us, including our feelings, desires, spirit, and body.

Finding Places of Community

But if we have isolated ourselves and tended not to trust people, how will we find community? Ideally, we will find a nurturing community within our local church, but some have learned to be quite guarded there. Unfortunately, it seems that sometimes wherever two or three are gathered—even in Jesus' name—there is *judgment* and *gossip* in the midst of them. Still, in friendships or groups within the church at large, we can find safe places to heal from denial, blame, isolation, and acting in anger. This community may take many forms.

A *friendship* in which two people are committed to each other and meet regularly can become a safe community.

Some *mentoring relationships* that are based on spiritual growth (although not necessarily the acquisition of ministry skills) work well as a community. In times past, Christians had spiritual directors or spiritual companions who listened to them and asked questions.

Small groups such as support groups, discipleship groups, Bible study groups and ministry teams work well when the focus of these groups is character formation. They mimic a nurturing family and provide safe settings in which people can work through struggles and character flaws.

Not every friendship, mentor relationship or small group can provide community. The participants need to build into the relationship the following qualities of community.

Safety

Confidentiality—not telling anyone else what is said—insures that we can reveal the worst secrets about ourselves without having them repeated. Trust cannot develop unless all comments are kept private.

Safe listening also involves hearing each other out without fixing each other. We don't offer opinions or give mini-sermons. We're careful to focus on truly listening to the person, not giving advice. We may tell how God worked in our lives, but we don't offer how-to steps to others. The Holy Spirit can convict others without anyone saying, You're a Christian. You shouldn't feel that way. Some groups practice safe listening with the "no cross talk" rule (no interrupting during a person's time to speak). This helps listeners too, especially if they've played the roles of Caretaker (Chapter 5) or Placater (Chapter 7). They learn to listen respectfully to others.

The safety of such relationships and groups lets us try out feelings we buried long ago. In the family role of the Adjuster (see Chapter 7), Anita never got angry even though she lived with a controlling husband and two rebellious teenage sons. In the safety of a support group, Anita tasted anger for the first time.

Several group members talked about how harshly their fathers spoke to them as children. I thought, What is their problem? Why didn't they tune it out?

Then someone repeated the exact phrase my dad used to say and I heaved a loud sigh. This was unusual because I'm the quiet one. Everyone looked at me in surprise.

The leader said, "Anita, do you want to be next?"

I sat quietly for a few minutes. I felt as if pine cones were growing in my throat and I couldn't

have talked even if I had wanted to. The tears be-
gan to flow.

Then I balled my hand into a fist and gently
pounded my knee. "Why did my father talk to me
that way?" I rasped. "I was such a good girl. I
never talked back to him like my sister did." I
couldn't quit crying and no one said anything for
several minutes.

I had never acted that way in the group before.
After the meeting, several people talked to me and
comforted me. At moments, I loved their comfort
and ate it up. At other moments, I hated it and
almost ran from the room. I forced myself to sit
through their encouragement. It was scary to be
angry. It was scary to be encouraged.

Anita's behavior may not seem angry compared to
more verbal expressions of anger, but to sweet, smiling
adjuster Anita, it was rage. Later that night, she again
recalled her childhood. When she allowed herself to
remember being sexually abused, her feet broke out in
welts. Anger was so foreign to her that her body reacted
to it. She was at last shattering the unwritten rules of her
family: don't speak up, don't let others encourage you,
and don't get angry. She knew that to get through this
anger, she needed to talk about it in the group the next
week. Anita continues:

I knew I couldn't speak out like the others, so I
wrote it down in a journal that I kept hidden. The
next week, I read the journal. As I finished, I start-
ed crying and the woman next to me put her arm
around me. I had always disliked being touched,
but that night I sank my head into the woman's lap
and cried for several minutes.

That was a turning point. Little by little, I began
to trust people. I could say what I thought without
fear of being attacked. I could let someone hug me
without hating it.

Honesty

A lot of before-and-after-church talk is the news, weather, and sports variety: "Did you see that big game yester-day?" or, "I like your new dress." We all find it difficult to talk about our faith and feelings.

Discussing confusion and anger can be refreshing, but sometimes it seems shocking and offensive to us. Others' stories challenge our mental ruts—are we struggling with the same shocking issue? Curt tells about one of his first support group experiences.

Everything was going well when the guy next to me (I'll call him Darrell) said: "I hate God."

I was shocked! No one else took it too hard though and, being a placater, I smiled at Darrell. At least he's honest, I thought.

I was also intrigued by the situation. There we sat on church-owned chairs in a church classroom and this guy said he hated God. Secretly, I had felt that same kind of anger at God, but I had never admitted it to anyone—especially in a church building! Boy, does this guy have guts, I thought.

Near the end of his sharing time, Darrell broke down in tears. He explained that he felt that God—in the form of his parents—had never reached out to him.

"My parents were so cold," he said. "They never told me they loved me. I felt alone and abandoned. They gave me money and everything I needed, but they never hugged me or touched me. I wasn't a bad kid. It wasn't fair that they ignored me."

I saw that something powerful was happening. These were honest people who were stating honest feelings and finding acceptance from other Christians. When my turn came, I mumbled that perhaps I had felt mad at God too. "Sometimes I don't understand the way He works," I told the group.

I rambled for a few minutes until I recalled the

Scripture that says that nobody understands the mind of God. ["Who has understood the mind of the LORD, or instructed Him as His counselor?" (Isa. 40:13)] As I talked, something happened. I felt some sense of relief. I was a little less angry and I began thinking that I could accept that I didn't understand God. This was the start of a more genuine relationship with him.

Darrell could have easily denied his anger toward God and wandered from faith. Instead, he found a place to talk about it. He knew he wanted to be close to God and this admission was the first step in understanding that God loved him. (We're not advocating a disrespect for God, but it's important to face ugly feelings so that our relationship with God can be healed.) Because Curt got to view this process, he dealt with the same problem as well. Looking back, Curt was stunned by the group's attitude:

The people in the group didn't act as if Darrell was worse than them because he said he was mad at God. They focused on their own situations. This honesty and acceptance created a place in which everyone could talk, trust and feel. People felt valued, and privileged to hear others confess their difficulties.

Can you imagine how upset people in many small groups would be if someone like Darrell shared that he hated God? He was afraid they would respond to him by saying, "I'll pray for you," or, "Let's talk to the pastor," or even, "The devil is after you. Claim the victory!" So Darrell kept quiet at church. Many Sundays he sat in church thinking he would explode if he didn't cry out to God. Darrell needed his fellow Christians to listen to his hurt and respond to it with God's unconditional love. If they had rushed in with platitudes about praying a little more and reading a little more Scripture, it would have been like a stone-faced nurse placing a Band-Aid on a patient with deep stab wounds. We all need more than bandaging, we need tenderness and recognition of our hurt.

Honesty seeps through the walls of denial and isolation that we have built around ourselves and helps us form close bonds with others. Most of us have let few people (and certainly not God) penetrate our walls. As we talk about deeper issues, we learn intimacy because we risk letting go of our fear of abandonment. As that fear diminishes, it's easier to risk connecting with God too.

Those who have experienced such honesty often become hooked on it—not because of its drama, but because of its healing. The heart feels refreshed because we see God working in our life. We realize that He can even replace those crazy feelings with a deep abiding love and trust for Him. By bonding together, we have the resources to show love and acceptance in a way that imitates the love of our Father.

You May Be Wondering . . .

Q *I'm between churches. How do I go about finding this sense of community?*

A First, stay in touch with people you already know. Close friends from the past can be helpful, even if means traveling or calling long distance to talk. Then lay this request for community before God and be sensitive to any promptings you may receive as you make an intense search for a friend or a group. Visit small groups at churches and, if you wish, a Twelve Step group of some kind (Adult Children of Alcoholics, Al-Anon, and so on). It wouldn't be unusual to find Christians there. As you scout around, keep your antenna out. Listen for comments that make a person sound safe. Invite that person or even several for coffee after a meeting or class and talk together for a while.

When looking for a church, call ahead and ask

questions about issues that are important to you (doctrine, style of worship, small groups). Look for others who are new because they'll be looking for friends too. Volunteer for a job that involves other people because working side by side is a quick way to get to know others. Keep an open mind because first impressions may be inaccurate.

Q *I told someone a secret in confidence and they told a group at church so they could pray about it. How am I supposed to trust anyone again?*

A Choose carefully the people to whom you want to reveal your feelings, thoughts, and motives and then ask their permission before doing so. Explain your past experience and say that you don't want to burden them with something they'll find too difficult to keep confidential. Explain what you mean by confidentiality—some people automatically figure it's OK to tell a spouse or even a prayer chain, when it may not be.

Realize also that the person who broke your confidence probably did not mean to hurt you intentionally. If you have not confronted that person, it would be helpful for you to talk to them and tell them how you feel.

Personal Reflection

Choose three or four of these questions and share the answers with a group or friend.

● Which story—Anita's or Darrell's—in this chapter sounds more interesting to you? Which one would have been more difficult for you to listen to if you had been a member of the group? Why?

● Who are the safe people or safe places in your life? What can you do to encourage these already existing relationships?

● Would you feel comfortable, or are you willing to risk, sharing the answers to these chapter-end questions with anyone? If so, who?

● How would you evaluate yourself as a listener? Circle a number on the left to indicate whether this statement about effective listening describes the way you behave:

often-1   sometimes-2   rarely-3   never-4

1	2	3	4	I try to listen without judgment.
1	2	3	4	I avoid giving opinions freely.
1	2	3	4	I avoid giving mini-sermons.
1	2	3	4	I monitor my feelings as a Caretaker or Placater.
1	2	3	4	I pray for a person when they tell me something that's difficult for them to say.

● Write a prayer, stating your greatest need in finding community.

● If you have not found a group or person with which to share the answers to some of the questions, please pray that God will help you find that safe place. Then, approach one person or attend one group to see if that may be His answer.

CHAPTER FOURTEEN

Admitting Who We Are

The frequent saying—"The church is not a hotel for saints, but a hospital for sinners"—hints at how we tend to behave like looking-good kids at church. This robs the church of a sense of community. A sense of community (true belonging) grows out of being able to reveal feelings that haven't been sanitized and still find acceptance. Confessing our faults to others teaches us how to talk, trust, and feel. This leads to healing, as the Scripture promises: "Therefore confess your sins to each other and pray for each other so that you may be healed. The prayer of a righteous man is powerful and effective" (James 5:16).

This kind of honesty was common in the early church's small groups: "The early Christian church cells were comprised of small groups of people who met regularly—often secretly. The order of worship was, first of all, self-disclosure and confession of sin. . . . This was followed by appropriate announcement of penance, pleas for forgiveness, and plans for making restitution. A final period of friendly fellowship (*koinonia*) closed the meeting."[1]

Yet confessing sins to each other isn't often talked about or put into action at church today. What is needed to make confession work among Christians?

Finding Safe Listeners

Because we see so little of confession, we're not sure how to do this. Confession is simply telling another about a fault, thought, or feeling we're not proud of. When properly understood, it can be integrated into Bible study groups, discipleship groups and relationships that seem safe. We often set aside time for prayer in these groups; we can also set aside time to state behaviors and attitudes for which we would like to be accountable.

When we look for people with whom we can build this kind of community, the principles from the last chapter apply: confidentiality, honesty, and humility. "Safe" people listen without playing preacher or armchair psychologist. They are aware of their own shortcomings, understanding that they have the potential of making the same mistake tomorrow that you are confessing today.

When they do speak, they act more like a cheerleader than an executioner. On the other hand, they don't brush our faults off with, "Everybody does that now and then." They believe in God's power to change you.

You may want to find "safe" people, using one of the following methods.

Look for honesty and faith

When Cynthia discovered that her husband of twenty years had been secretly bisexual, she hated him. Cynthia needed to confess this hatred and promise to work through it, but she didn't know who could handle such sensational news. She chose her Bible study leader, Martha, for two reasons. First, Martha often admitted her own faults to the group. And, Martha prayed a lot. Cynthia knew that Martha could help her lean on God's power.

Test the waters

Reveal something less significant and see how people react. When Patty first attended a support group, she didn't trust that the people would accept her. So she mentioned how bad she felt for yelling at her kids earlier that day, and then watched the group members. They didn't know it, but she was testing them. They "passed" in several ways. One was that when others talked, they mentioned their struggles with that problem, what they thought were at the root of it and what they were doing about it. She also noticed that after the group, no one said, "Patty, if you would just read this book. . . ." Before she left, she and another mother agreed to pray for each other and call each other for encouragement.

Recall previous comments

When Bob and his wife divorced, they disappeared from church. When a couple from church invited Bob for dinner, he spilled his story and his fault in the break up. Bob told them that he knew they were "safe" because in a conversation several years before, the wife said that it grieved her that people were so hard on divorced friends who were already hurting.

Christian growth is too important to be insensitive to others and waste time being spiritual frauds. How much better to seek out "safe" listeners and set ourselves on a path of growth.

Acknowledging Guilt

Another reason we don't easily admit mistakes is that guilt doesn't feel good. It can also be difficult to figure out what exactly to feel guilty for. Those of us who are caretakers assume that much of what happens is our fault. In admitting our wrongs, we need to take responsibility for what we did wrong, and leave the rest alone. I clean up my side of the street, so to speak, but I can't clean up someone else's side. For example, if someone blows up at you, you are responsible for how you respond. If you respond without harshness (even though you may have been firm), you don't have to take responsibility for the other person's blowing up. If you pushed that person until he blew up, you need to admit being pushy and apologize for that. You don't, however, take responsibility for his blowing up.

Taking responsibility for what we haven't done is false guilt. True guilt tells us that we *did* something wrong and we need to ask for forgiveness. False guilt (or shame) is that miserable feeling that tells us we *are* wrong to the core. It makes itself plain in thoughts such as: *I not only made a mistake, I am a mistake; if something goes wrong, I must be the cause.* Besides plummeting our self-worth, false guilt edges out the role of true guilt. If we are steeped in shame, we don't become convicted by true guilt, confess it and find forgiveness. There is no reprieve for shame.

When we confess, we mention the part for which we are guilty. If we're unsure of what our part is, we can talk about the situation with a friend and ask God to show us our part. Then we confess our fault without mentioning the other party's fault. We leave that on their side of the street for them to clean up.

Accountability

One rich advantage of confessing our faults to someone we trust is that a mild accountability exists. We confess out loud that we exaggerated our achievements on a résumé, that we called ourselves "Stupid!" for dropping a pen, that we held a loved one at a distance because we fear his or her abandonment of us. Even though the hearer of our confession accepts us, we think twice before repeating the mistake. We have a partner now on our spiritual journey and we can rely on their help. We would also rather not admit this fault again to the same person or group. We feel a gentle accountability toward them.

We may even choose to make ourselves accountable to a person or group: "If I'm tempted to . . . I will call you." When we make ourselves accountable, it's wise to come up with reasonable and practical steps to overcome behaviors. Charlotte tells her story:

> *I felt attracted to a married man, and even though I felt ashamed I couldn't stop the feeling. So I confessed it to a mentor friend, Helen. She listened and acknowledged that she had struggled the same way a few times.*
>
> *Then Helen said, "What are you going to do about it?"*
>
> *"I have to stop fantasizing," I replied.*
>
> *"Does that seem possible at the moment?" Helen asked me. I admitted that it didn't.*
>
> *"Do you think it would help if you substituted the fantasy with another activity?" Helen asked. "I tried praying for the man instead of fantasizing! I sure couldn't do both at the same time!"*
>
> *I liked Helen's idea and I talked with her about what was at the root of the attraction. We figured out it might be my marital troubles. My husband and I were working on our relationship, but I felt unloved a lot of the time.*
>
> *"What if, when I'm drawn into the fantasy, I think about how much God loves me?" I asked Helen. She thought that was a good idea and I could hear her thumbing through her Bible. Finally, she gave me a verse to meditate on: "God loves me and delights in me" (an adaptation of Ps. 147:11). I agreed to check in with Helen every other day on my progress and she agreed to pray for me. After a week or so, the fantasizing stopped, which helped me work on my marriage.*

Charlotte and Helen's talk helped Charlotte for several reasons.

- Helen listened to Charlotte without judgment.
- Helen admitted having experienced the same temptation.

- Helen offered a suggestion without insisting that Charlotte take it. This freed Charlotte to use it as a spring board to seek God's direction on what would work best for her.
- Charlotte's goal was ownable and reachable. She didn't promise to stop fantasizing, only to redirect her thoughts.
- Charlotte promised to report to Helen, who agreed to pray for her.

Their conversation illustrates well the mutuality of confession and the way Christian community provides a hospital for sinners, sometimes even an intensive care ward.

How Confession in Community Helps
Confession helps us understand
the messages we send ourselves

As we examine why we do what we do, scenes replay themselves from our past. We aren't even conscious of how we react to certain people who behave in ways similar to our parent. As we talk about it in a safe relationship, these things come to light and can be more easily surrendered to God. This helps us face our real selves, and find healing and make better choices based on what we truly think and feel.

Confession relieves anxiety

Once these feelings are out in the light, we don't feel so bound by them. Because secrecy is part of what makes them so overwhelming, revealing them reduces anxiety and loneliness.

Confession empowers us

Because we've told the secret and found acceptance, the hidden behavior, feeling or situation loses its powerful grip on us. It has felt scary to harbor secret doubts about whether God is watching over us or not, secret fears that we will never find approval or affirmation, and secret anger that life is so disappointing. We want to shake them. Hearing that others experience these things frees us to examine them and work them out with God.

Confession can invite appropriate affection

Revealing our true selves may send us into the embrace of a good friend whom we can trust. Friends, mentors and support group members can be these physical arms of God, letting us know that we are loved and valued.

Confession helps us set limits on the King Baby in us

We listen to ourselves talk and discover our impatience: *That group member is boring. I wish he would keep quiet*—that sounds really harsh, doesn't it? Sometimes, we back up and reword our extreme emotions. *I felt like killing her*—no, I don't mean that at all—she just irritated me. Because we hear our words spoken out loud, it's easier to reword things. We can own our emotions, switching from *His complaining drives me crazy* to *I tend to get irritated by people who complain a lot.* We try to offer others the same grace and mercy that we're receiving from the safe relationship.

Even with all these benefits, accountability terrifies most of us. In the beginning, it feels terrible. The first few times you confess a fault to someone, it feels as if a volcano were erupting inside you. After a while, it's more like the prick of a needle. It's practically nothing compared to the tremendous relief that follows. After you become used to having a clean conscience, a secret hurts more than confession ever will.

Fears That Hold Us Back

It's normal to feel afraid to open up about mistakes and hurts. Even when we confess only to safe persons who will accept us and keep our words confidential, we wonder.

Fear of hurt

We step out slowly, being patient with what we're able to reveal. We may have to reassure ourselves over and over that we will survive.

Fear of rejection

The great fear in confessing a fault, hidden feeling or disgusting habit is that the hearer will think less of me. Many people, however, have the same feelings we have and they're relieved to find that others have feet of clay. We mistakenly believe that others have their lives in order and it's only we who don't. The more transparent we are, the more others are likely to trust us.

Rejection is inevitable. We face it by admitting our hurt. As we talk about it with someone else, we may see what we did wrong or perhaps that the assessment of the one who rejected us is not accurate. Besides, we still have the reassurance of those we're learning to trust.

Jan tells how being a judgmental listener convicted her.

In a support group several years ago, an embarrassed woman confessed that she yelled at her daughter's teacher. I said nothing, but I kept thinking how immature that woman was. The next day, my son's teacher was unfair with him as she had been twice before. I found myself holding the telephone, ready to call the teacher and the principal, and I was so mad I probably would have yelled at the teacher.

I remembered the woman in the group and thought, I am doing the thing I criticized her for. There, but for the grace of God, go I! I toned down what I said to the principal and we made some progress in solving the problem. After the call, I prayed for myself and for her and vowed not to be so judgmental. When I feel critical of someone, I often remember that woman and step back from judging.

Fear of memories

Those who suffered physical or sexual abuse often block feelings because they fear they will remember traumatic events they've tried to forget. Some abuse victims have blocked specific early childhood memories to protect themselves, so when memories do surface, they may come in pieces. Some people remember only smells or sounds but dreams or conversations bring back more of the memory. Even then, many people aren't sure if what they remember is true, even though they recall vivid details and remember them while they're fully awake. We have to trust that God will help us remember what our conscious mind is equipped to face at the appropriate time.

Even those who weren't abused often shut out the trauma of childhood. A simple feeling surfaces and overwhelms us and we're not sure why. As an adult, Candace visited her parents whom she had not seen in several years.

My parents figured I would sleep in the same bedroom I had slept in as a teenager. When I was alone in that room, all those old feelings of depression and hopelessness overwhelmed me. I remembered sitting on the floor of my bedroom as a teenager listening to my parents argue, thinking that I would never find peace. I used to turn up the stereo so I couldn't hear anything.

Even though I was now an adult, I clung to my pillow throughout the night as I slept. I was already worried about my job and being in my old bedroom made me more insecure than ever. The next night I made an excuse to stay in another room.

This experience helped me because I was in denial about my childhood. I kept telling a group I attend for my bulimia that it hadn't been all that bad. I see now that I felt hopeless as an adolescent. That hopelessness feeds into my current craze of thinness and acceptance by others.

It takes courage to endure the hurt of some memories. When we accept this challenge, we find that God can sustain us and love us as much as if He were physically holding us in His arms and loving us. He doesn't want us to stay locked in the closet forever.

Hearing The Confessions of Others

When friends confess their mistakes or group members pour out deep woes, we can feel honored that we're considered safe enough to receive their confession. While others talk about their pick for the Super Bowl, those of us within communities of faith and safety can allow people to reveal their struggles. Jan felt honored to receive someone's confession this way:

A single friend who had moved away called me long distance in tears. I listened, as she stumbled and struggled to talk. Finally it came out: she was lonely and she had slept with a man.

Rather than interrupting her or trying to fix her (as had been my custom in the past), I remained quiet. Because she had a strong commitment to Christ, I knew that she was repentant and full of sorrow. After she unloaded her story, we talked about how much God loved her and that only He could fulfill her need for love in that faraway city. We talked about how she could avoid falling into this problem in the future. Then we prayed together.

After we hung up, I thanked God for the telephone call. I thanked Him that this woman had received many of my confessions before. I thanked Him that she had called me with this confession instead of burying it. I thanked Him for the honor of being a hearer of that confession, and I prayed for her. I also thanked Him for the many people He had put in my path who had heard my confessions, and set such an example of God's grace and mercy for me.

You May Be Wondering . . .

Q *How is confession different from dumping our troubles on other people?*

A Disclosing our real selves to others resembles dumping because we feel such relief. If the listener is someone with similar experiences, we also sense a commonality with them that relieves our isolation. The big difference between confession and dumping is that confession carries with it the goal to grow and mature in Christ. It's a matter of saying, "This is who I am now, but I want to be what God wants me to be."

Wise mentors and friends may even ask, "What are you going to do about this?" This is not to press them to come up with a formula, but to plant a seed of seeking wholeness. When people dump their troubles, they're looking for a sympathy but not healing. There's no seeking God's will for resolution to the problem.

Q *The Bible states clearly that Jesus is the only mediator between God and man, so doesn't confession of sin to others put them in the place of Christ?*

A Christians receive forgiveness of sins from God through Jesus Christ, the only mediator: "For there is one God and one mediator between God and men, the man Christ Jesus, who gave Himself as a ransom for all men — the testimony given in its proper time" (1 Tim. 2:5-6). This chapter does not describe how we receive forgiveness through Christ (though it is implied), but how God heals us: "Therefore confess your sins to each other and pray for each other so that you may be healed" (James 5:16). The reciprocal relationship of Christians confessing their sins to each other eliminates the idea that any one person is more than another in God's eyes. Ideally, those who hear our confession are the same ones whose faults we know well because they have confessed their sins to us.

Personal Reflection

Choose three or four of these questions and share the answers with a group or friend.

● How do you respond to this verse? "Therefore confess your sins to each other and pray for each other so that you may be healed" (James 5:16).

● Who do you consider safe enough to confess your mistakes to? What makes you consider them safe? How would you approach them?

● Describe a time you felt relieved to find out that someone else made the same mistake you made.

● What are your fears about confession and accountability? Who could you talk with about them?

CHAPTER FIFTEEN

Creating Safe Places

Imagine someone sitting next to a lake reading a Bible with eyebrows furrowed and hands clasped. Doesn't that look like someone absorbed in self-examination? It does occur in this setting, but as it becomes a pattern of life it can occur in chaotic board meetings or in the kitchen chopping vegetables. Listening to God's voice becomes a round-the-clock adventure. Here are descriptions of a few familiar tools to use to explore and express feelings and motives, to see how they square with reality and to what God's will is regarding them.

Letting Go in Safe Places

Because our culture views solitude as a waste of time, many people fill up free nights and weekends. Self-examination, however, requires solitude, which can provide safe settings in which we interact with God using these tools.

Cry freely

Even though tears have been taboo in our culture of strong, rugged individualists, the humility of self-examination allows us the freedom to cry. Our culture says that crying means we're weak, unstable and out of control, but in reality crying can provide strength and stability as we let go of frustrations. Researchers studying crying have discovered that tears are one of the body's waste-disposal systems, which explains why crying frees us from tension and keeps us from going over the edge.[1] A good cry releases the pressure in our holding tanks and allows hurt, anger, and fear to escape. It breaks up the intensity of our self-examination work and may even relieve headaches and muscle tension. Crying is a preliminary step to laughing and trusting.

Tears are often a sign that our feelings are coming alive again. They are good for the soul because they can be prayers — the most honest prayers many of us have ever prayed. They express feelings we can't put into words.

While many prefer to cry in private, sharing tears can be like spilling perfume. Its healing fragrance reaches others who are touched and freed as well. The tears we shed alone in God's presence can commemorate our rebonding with Him, if we may have distanced ourselves from Him in the past.

Journaling

Journals are safe places to confess and work through answers to the questions: "How do I feel? What do I think? What will I do?" In the privacy of a journal we can admit our true feelings. There's no one to offend, so we can speak honestly. We may even wish to address all or part of the journal to God. Since our thoughts are written down, we can re-read them to see if we blamed someone or denied feelings. Then we can rephrase what we've written until we're no longer blaming anyone. The more honest we are in a journal, the more genuine our relationship with God will be. This excerpt from Curt's journal illustrates this:

Today I met with Terry. It amazes me how the last time we met he seemed so depressed with so many difficult things going on in his life. I remember thinking, I'm glad my life is going better than that! *Now the tables have turned. I'm struggling and he's helping me. God, I continue to learn about humility and true friendship. I hope I don't have to learn this again—but I probably will!*

Many people shy away from journaling because they've encumbered it with so many rules. The grammar in a journal may be garbled and the penmanship a mere scribble, but the feelings can be honest. Although some journal each day, we can journal as needed, which may be weekly, bi-weekly, or monthly. Whatever the pattern, we keep alert for moments when we feel the urge to confess, to grieve, to rejoice, to surrender as ripe moments for journaling.

Many people find it helpful to journal in a special place such as a favorite chair or a bench in the backyard. Studies suggest that the more special the setting, the better. "Try to find a room where you will not be interrupted or bothered by unwanted sounds, sights or smells," says psychologist Dr. James Pennebaker in his book, *Opening Up The Healing Power of Confiding in Others.*[2] If you think someone will be tempted to look at your journal, keep it in a locked drawer or briefcase.

Prayer As a Way of Life

While prayer outlines and request lists are helpful in prayer, we can also enjoy the simplicity of praying all day. We go in and out of prayer as the day stretches before us, basking in the love, comfort and conviction of God who never forsakes us. To wait in a doctor's office is a chance to reconnect with our greatest source of love and affirmation. A talk with a friend is a chance to surrender that person to God.

Our pattern of self-examination helps us learn to sit quietly before God. We may meditate on a Bible verse or see ourselves as participants in a passage of the Gospels.

We wait in silence for these truths to soak in as we lay them before God with this question: "What is it You wish to say to me through this passage?" We don't worry if the answer doesn't appear billboard-style in our minds. We can wait for it to come through ordinary events in life.

Gut Level Prayer

It's a mistake to assume prayer is a tidy offering of well-chosen words. While those kinds of prayers are valuable, so are the ones that make little sense to others. Consider Hannah whose words were so slurred and gestures so exaggerated that the Old Testament priest Eli mistook her for a drunk. Like her, we can find release in "pouring out [our] soul to the Lord" (1 Sam. 1:15b). We can reveal our ugly feelings and far-fetched conclusions.

We know we're in good company because King David of the Old Testament did the same. Many of the Psalms begin as "rag sessions" of depression, doubt, and even revenge (Pss. 6:6; 31:1; 55:15) — but they end in praise. We can copy this pattern, ranting to God so that in His presence we can look at our motives and bitter feelings. This method gives us a sense that God sees beyond our childish behavior to us, His children who need His grace. But is this irreverent? If God wasn't offended when David expressed honest feelings and He even let David's words be incorporated into the canon of the Holy Scriptures, surely we can be as honest.

An unusual form of gut-level prayer is to write a letter of confrontation to people who have hurt you. Scribble it out, read it to God, but don't send it. If you think you wish to send a form of it, ask God to show you what exactly to say.

Enjoying God
Sing about God's love

Many hymns, Scripture songs, and simple childhood songs reassure us that God loves us. Singing "Jesus

Loves Me" tells us that we too are the "little ones" that belong to Jesus. It's OK that we are weak, because He is strong. This song like many others helps us understand that God affirms us, loves us, and holds us in our frustration and pain.

If we have found a safe relationship or group within our church, we have the additional joy of singing together in corporate worship and recognizing how certain phrases (e.g., about trust or God's love) coincide to what we've said when we're together. At a conference which included small group sharing, 800 joined hands and sang, "Jesus Loves Me." As adults reaching out to God, we absorbed the truth of that song in a new way. Several were moved to tears as one said he felt for the first time that Jesus was holding and loving his real self that only He knew.

Make worship an important part of your life

If we have imagined God to be a tyrant, we can realign our view by relishing the songs and hymns that emphasize God's greatness, His love, His forgiveness. Worship is a powerful vehicle to negate the shame we have experienced. It moves us beyond the cognitive level of understanding and helps us believe in our hearts that God is a capable and powerful parent. For some, meaningful worship means singing more songs in the car or in the shower. These private times of worship help us enter even more into worship services at church.

Picture God's love

By personalizing Psalms, we can figuratively crawl into God's lap and have him hold us and rock us to sleep:

> *He reached down from on high and took hold of me;*
> *He drew me out of deep waters. . . .*
> *He brought me out into a spacious place;*
> *He rescued me because He delighted in me.*
>
> Psalm 18:16, 19

Here's another vehicle that Jan uses to picture God's love for her.

A child development specialist advised me to buy a picture of Jesus holding a child on his lap for my daughter so that she would understand that God loves her. In the picture I bought her, Jesus touches the child so gently and holds His hand behind her head. He rubs His bearded cheek next to her cheek and she looks peaceful. Sometimes when I have failed or I feel lonely, I take this picture down from my daughter's wall, bring it to work with me and set it behind my computer monitor. Throughout the day, I look at it and picture myself as the child. I think about how God loves me the same way and it comforts me.

Creative pursuits

Cindy doesn't see herself as an artistic person, but in the loneliness of her eventual divorce she sketched pictures when she felt the urge to buy a romance novel. Many times she drew a woman sitting in a corner alone in a chair. "Even though I felt completely alone, I tried to picture the truth by penciling in a mist around the woman to represent God. This helped me see that God loves me and has a purpose for me. I need to know that."

Managing Pain and Frustration

When we've listened to our feelings and done all the self-examination we're capable of, we may still feel miserable. We know enough not to spill that misery on others, but how can we ventilate these feelings without striking out at the people we love? By building healthy escapes into our lives on a regular basis. These include physical activities such as running, race walking, roller skating, aerobic exercising, or playing basketball. (On particularly stressful days, it may help to whack away at a punching bag, throw pillows, or scream into a pillow.) For others, the fine arts provide a helpful escape. Playing a piano or trumpet helps us exhale our frustration. Looking through a book of reproductions of great paintings or reading a book of poetry or a children's picture book can speak to the depth of the soul to provide release and reassurance.

Serve from a Full Heart

As we identify how we do things to placate other people or to draw attention to ourselves, we can re-examine our service. If our motives for certain forms of service are self-seeking and we can't seem to realign them, we need to shed that area of service and find one that God lays on our heart. Then we are free to discover what it means to serve one another in love (Gal. 5:13). Does this sound too difficult? As we recognize our own ego's nudge for attention, we can tell the difference between it and God's nudges tugging on our hearts. Jan tells this story about those nudges at war within us.

> *One night as I was setting up chairs to lead a support group in my church, I began wondering if anyone remembered how I showed up faithfully every Wednesday night to lead this group. Then I remembered that in the last church directory, our group had been left out of the list of ministries! That did it. I decided to write a note to the pastor about anything I could think of and leave it for him. I'd start it out with, "While I was here leading the support group Wednesday night, . . ." That would remind him that our group did exist and that I showed up faithfully to lead it.*
>
> *I almost wrote the note. Then I saw my partner in leadership drive up and I thought about how she had asked me to start the group. I had resisted in the beginning, fearful that I was back to my old excuse-me-while-I-save-the-world approach to life. But I kept telling her how much a group had*

helped me, so she asked me to start one and she would help.

I looked at my friend coming up the cement walk and I looked at the empty chairs that would soon be filled with people admitting their deepest fears. "I can't write the note," I said aloud to God. I knew that I had started the group because God had led me to do it. I knew that He was using it to help others, as well as my friend and me. I would ask the secretary to be sure we were included in the next directory, but I could not taint this service with my old pattern of needing to be noticed.

Some who are taking this journey of self-examination come away feeling they aren't worthy to serve. The truth is that wounded people in the process of healing are well equipped to serve. They are in the process of facing their deeper motives and clearing out egotistical cries within themselves. They are learning to hear more clearly God's cry within them and they're equipped to follow it.

Play
Use childlike comforts

On occasion, members of the support group to which Curt belonged would bring teddy-bears to meetings. Other members thought it was unusual at first. Curt finally talked to them about it.

I didn't know what to say to the women who brought the teddy-bears, so I asked, "What's his name?" They gave their teddy-bears cute names like Cuddles and Buffy. Some of these stuffed animals were twenty years old and had ragged red ribbons or only one eye. I was embarrassed for these women—they were my friends. Can't you leave them in the car? *I thought.*

Finally I saw that there was something special going on. As these women talked in the group about their upbringing, the teddy-bears helped them talk. It sounds funny, but it was as if they held the teddy-bears as they would like to have been held. Once I got over being embarrassed, I realized I was jealous because they returned to their childhood method of comfort so easily. I began wondering what would help me do the same thing.

Indulge in childlike play

As we let go of the tension pervading our lives, we may delight in activities we loved as children such as climbing trees, playing with yo-yos, or drawing with colored pens. Childlike play provides a needed balance of relaxation to the demanding schedule of life. This is especially important during intense times of self-examination. We need a rest from the hard work of stepping on the brakes of our behavior patterns, grinding them to a halt and moving in reverse. We can reward ourselves with "down time" in childlike play.

Professional Help

Those who struggle with being transparent about feelings and do not have a reliable support system may need professional help to understand the effects of their upbringing. This is especially true if you find yourself dealing with excessive anger and repressed memories of physical or sexual abuse. Therapists are trained to create a safe environment for the real self to question, to weep, or to get angry. They help people monitor and manage rage in a crisis.

Therapists can also help in a crisis because they recognize physical disorders, deep psychological hurt, or true suicidal intentions. Some find that investing time and money in therapy makes them more accountable and keeps them from denying they have a problem.

Counseling provides the one-on-one attention that some did not receive while growing up. It's a chance to receive someone else's focused attention, to be fully heard. Those who have never trusted anyone can know that in a therapist they have someone who is legally bound to confidentiality.

You May Be Wondering . . .

Q *Isn't it unhealthy for my children to see me cry?*
A Our tears may make a spouse, friends, or children feel uncomfortable because they feel as if our sorrow is their fault or that they have to help us. It's wise to explain that our crying has nothing to do with their behavior, but that it's a positive release of sad feelings. This is a healthy model for children. To relieve their anxiety further, we can choose to cry in private.

Q *How do I choose a counselor?*
A Get recommendations from friends, support group members, and counseling centers at churches. Look for a counselor who is a committed Christian, working through his or her childhood issues. Check also to see what the counselor's licenses and credentials are and what your health insurance covers.

When you find a possible candidate, ask for a consultation. To understand their approach to treatment, you might ask, "How do you work with clients to overcome problems such as the one I have?" Ask also about their specific training and previous experiences and specializations.

Most people prefer a therapist they "click with." See if you're comfortable with their personality, age, gender, marital status, and denominational preference. When we are working through the pain of a particular trauma such as abuse, we may prefer a therapist who has worked through the same issues.

Gender is important to many. If you want to work out problems with your father, it may help to see a male therapist. You may not be ready to do this if you were abused by your father, in which case a female therapist might be better.

Personal Reflection

Choose three or four of these questions and share the answers with a group or friend.

● How do you feel about crying freely? Journaling?

● In what unusual moments and places do you pray? What are some other moments or places in which you could enjoy God's presence even though you're involved in another activity?

● In what ways did you play or relax as a child? Do you still do any of these things today? If not, would you like to?

● What healthy escapes do you currently use? (talking with a friend, running, race walking, roller skating, aerobic exercising, riding a bike, whacking at a punching bag, throwing pillows, playing a musical instrument, looking through a book of art, reading a book of poetry.) Name another you could try.

● Buy yourself something you loved in childhood—a jump rope, a set of colored pens, even a toy train. Set aside some time to enjoy using it. Comment here about your experiences with it.

Part IV
Tools for Building Resilience

CHAPTER SIXTEEN

Moving toward Stability

Ups and downs are normal in our path of Christian growth, and especially so when we're bold and honest enough to look at our real selves. We may be patient with a troublesome person one day and sharp the next. The overall movement is upward even though we become overwhelmed and resort to old behaviors at times.

Resilient Christians

The quality that separated biblical heroes from other biblical figures was that their faith gave them the endurance to bounce back. Peter denied Jesus three times and felt enormous guilt, but he sought Jesus out and received forgiveness. Judas betrayed Jesus, felt enormous guilt, and hung himself. Peter and other biblical heroes weren't perfect, but they kept interacting with God even when they made mistakes. If we can add endurance to our faith, we'll be able to withstand pressure and recover from setbacks.

Some people are more resilient than others due to individual personalities, past experiences, and biological and physiological make up. Resiliency can, however, be built into the character when people learn to manage life's difficulties. Walking the journey we're describing in this book builds that strength and resiliency because we're more likely to bounce back from the stress points in life if we've developed more authentic relationships with God and others.

Potential Hazards on The Journey

When we know our patterns from the past, it's easier to spot potential pitfalls and prepare ourselves for them. Here are a few to consider.

Physical depletion

During stressful times, the body is drained of energy. We can renew our bodies with adequate sleep and the healing effects of crying, laughter and exercise. We who take ourselves too seriously need to laugh down to the bone and completely lose our composure.

At the first sign of a crisis or life transition, we check our balance—are we taking care of ourselves and using our tools? On days when we feel as if we can do nothing right, we ask ourselves the HALT questions: "Am I Hungry, Angry, Lonely, or Tired?" Ileana checked herself this way.

> *I was already angry with a coworker because she implied to my boss that I wasn't pulling my share of the workload. Then my friend Letitia called to cancel our lunch date. She had a valid excuse—she had to go home and check on her sick daughter. Letitia said she was sorry and I knew she had a valid reason to cancel, but I still felt abandoned. See, no one wants to be my friend anyway, I thought to myself. I couldn't shake the anger and loneliness.*
>
> *I decided I would go out for ice cream during my lunch hour—I would get one of those huge sundaes. Then I would feel better.*
>
> *Then I thought of the HALT saying. No wonder I wanted to "pig out." I was angry at my coworker*

and lonely for a friend.

Let's sort this out, *I thought.* How I can get my needs met legitimately? *First, I talked with my boss and corrected what my co-worker said. (My boss had suspected the truth already.) Then I called Letitia and said, "I know you need to check on your daughter, but can I ride along with you? This is one of those days I need to be with a friend." That was fine with Letitia and we enjoyed our time together.*

Stuck in anger

Anger can be motivating, especially when it forces us out of denial. But when we replay past events in our minds and become stuck in them, our anger uses us instead of our using it. Then we become hopeless, feeling that God can't help us overcome destructive feelings and patterns. Holding on to our anger slows down our progress because we put energy into anger that should be channeled into seeking God (Eph. 4:26, 31). To avoid this, we express our anger in safe ways by crying, journaling, exercising, shouting where safe to do so, talking to an understanding friend, writing those unmailed letters—whatever helps us work through our anger without harming others.

Plateaus of fear

If we need to take a step forward but shrink from it, we're likely to sit on the roadside of our journey. Perhaps it's time to be assertive in a relationship, to forgive a friend, to face out-of-control spending habits, but this seems too difficult. When we can use our tools to work up the courage to take the necessary risk, we break through the inertia of the plateau.

Blaming family

Living a life filled with, "If only my mother hadn't . . ." and, "It's my brother's fault that I . . ." keeps us from taking personal responsibility for our own growth. It chains us to bitterness and immaturity.

Besides, blaming parents is unfair because many times they did rather well in spite of their own culture and upbringing. If we knew the dilemmas they faced as children, we might be surprised at how well they did. Recovering alcoholics at Alcoholics Anonymous meetings often talk about how they tried to be good parents but how badly they blew it. They love their children and wish they had been more nurturing (which is a familiar feeling to *all* parents). Perhaps these thoughts are your parents' thoughts as well. This doesn't erase the effects of their behavior on us as adults, but it does mean that blame is inappropriate.

In an effort to do the right thing, Christians may force themselves to forgive parents. This backfires because anger comes back. It helps to view forgiveness as both a *goal* and a *process*. We accept that we are in the process of forgiveness as we ask God to help us achieve the goal of forgiveness. We head toward that goal and understand that forgiveness is often a by-product of working through repressed feelings and anger. After we have done this, we know what we are forgiving and forgiveness comes from the depths of us. In the meantime, we fluctuate between anger and acceptance. Here are Glenn's experiences:

> At Thanksgiving, my relatives put eight bottles of wine on the table even though my brothers drink too much. Instead of wondering when they'd learn, I finally accepted this. They aren't interested in changing and I'm not going to change them.
>
> Sometimes I don't do so well. Our family has a pattern of using subtle guilt and shame to get us to conform to family wishes. I can't stand it after a while and I make an excuse to leave. I don't want to be unkind, so I would rather leave than get angry.

Accepting parents means we quit trying to change them. If they're workaholics or rage-aholics, we do little good trying to persuade them to address these issues. (Nevertheless, a formal intervention for alcoholic or drug addicted parents done by an entire family with the help of a professional is a worthwhile effort.)

We would do well to sit before God in solitude and weigh these questions:

- Am I as far down the road to forgiveness as I can be at this moment?
- Am I honestly praying for my parents and wishing God's best for them—love, joy, peace, patience, and so on?
- Am I acknowledging how hard they did try and the obstacles they overcame?

Nothing spectacular may come to us in those quiet moments, but little by little God moves us farther down the path of forgiveness. As our acceptance of our parents grows, we explore the possibility of having a new relationship with them. We don't expect them to be Superdad or Supermom, but they are normal people who have struggled. They are also people with whom we have much in common, people that we love.

Family get-togethers

Holidays are happy for some people, but many others feel lonely and sad at those times (what some call the "holiday blues"). If you're changing the way you're relating to people, it can be scary to face a family get-together. New patterns of relating to people can confuse and even alienate relatives. It's as if you're singing a new song and they don't like its style.

Consider each invitation carefully. You may even want to remain non-committal until you have time to think it through. Your goal is to be the same person all the time, saying and acting as you truly are, but also considering what would be the kind and loving thing to do. Allow God to lead you in this thought process by asking yourself:

- Do I want to do this?
- Am I equipped to be my true self with these people or will I revert to my old patterns?
- Am I being shamed into this?
- Do I have other commitments that are more important for that time slot?
- Is there a third option—a compromise, perhaps?

When we're struggling with a particularly dominant relative, we may even have to take a year off from family outings. Maggie skipped the family Thanksgiving dinner because she knew that her uncle would be there. He had abused her as a child and she was too angry at him to see him without creating a scene. Dennis had never worked up the courage to tell his parents that he didn't like pulling his children away from their presents on Christmas morning and driving several hours to their house. He finally did and his parents got upset. By the time he and his family saw his parents a week later, they had discovered they liked spreading out the celebrations as well. Sometimes it helps to talk to a friend as Carla did.

My father called to say that he wanted to visit—he had even made his reservations already. He planned to stay two weeks! What could I do?

I told him I would have to check my schedule. I hung up and called my friend, Gail. Gail quizzed me gently. "Do you want to see him? Can you handle it?"

"Yes, but not for two weeks."

"How long do you want to see him?" Gail asked.

"Two days is about what I can handle."

"Could you suggest he stay for only two days? You could say that two days will work best for you. You don't have to explain yourself."

That's what I did and the visit went well. I love my father, but I don't yet know how to respond to him. Normally I let him push my buttons, but this shorter visit was a good experience for us.

Talking with Concerned People

Beware of well-intentioned, but uninformed advice givers who tell you their version of what God wants you to do. Without knowing anything about your struggle or distance from God or pent-up emotions, they may push you to forget the past, take control of your life and move on before you are ready. But if they continue to press you, you may want to say, "I'm working on some issues in my life that are helping me understand myself better."

Helpfulness is the measure of how much to say. If talking with parents will help your relationship with them in some way, consider it. Jeanette wanted to talk to her parents but didn't know how. She told them a little at a time. When they asked her repeatedly to help them out but didn't ask the other children, she explained, "I will help, but I'm not the family hero, Mom. The other kids in this family can help too." When her mother tried to get her to talk to her brother about reconciling with his wife, Jeanette said, "I'm not the mediator between with you and him anymore. If you want to tell him something, call him." She loved her mother a great deal and found it difficult to say these things, but she found that taking a deep breath and a using a gentle tone of voice helped immensely.

Some people, especially those who were physically or sexually abused, believe it's important to confront their parents about past behaviors. Motives for doing so can be difficult to sort out. Sometimes it's done with subtle feelings of revenge: *They hurt me, now I'll hurt them.* Seeking revenge shows that we are stuck in anger and not focusing on our own side of the street. We need to ask, *Why am I doing this? What do I hope to accomplish?*

Those who come from families in which the problems were particularly discreet may still find confrontation helpful, but a little more difficult. Perhaps the family was respected and admired publicly or one child was abused by a parent but no one admitted it. This helps the person come out of denial and believe that he or she needs to look at the past.

If you believe that talking with your family will cause more dissension than you can face, it might be as helpful to talk to someone besides parents, such as aunts, uncles or grandparents who are more open. The important thing is to speak the truth and have it validated.

It's also possible to confront parents indirectly. Some write their thoughts in a journal or even in a letter, but never send it. Others confront their parents by telling a support group what they would like to say to a parent. Even though the parents aren't present, anger is released, the truth is revealed and the person is one step closer to healing.

You May Be Wondering . . .

Q *Why is there so much talk about being a victim today?*

A People who have struggled throughout their lives often blame themselves for everything. It can be a relief to understand they weren't responsible for all of it, but that they were victims of difficult situations who may have responded the best they could.

As aware and informed adults, however, they have choices. The best choice is to take responsibility for their behaviors by seeking God's path for healing. That means that even though the issues discussed in this book may sometimes be painful to examine, they do so anyway. They refuse to be victims.

To remain a victim means to remain angry, blaming, and isolating and bound to the mistakes of the past. A resilient person overcomes the past by examining it and its effects on them and learning new ways of responding.

Q *Do I still need to look at how the past affects me if my parents are deceased? What difference does it make?*

A The death of a parent(s) doesn't diminish the effect that upbringing had on you as a child, but it does create extra challenges as an adult. Our culture tends to deify dead persons, so you may feel guilty for thinking of deceased parents as anything less than saintly. Siblings may particularly resent your looking at the past because they have glorified your parents and reprogrammed their own memories. Give yourself permission to work through the anger and hurt. In time, you will be more at peace than ever with your memory of them.

Personal Reflection

Choose three or four of these questions and share the answers with a group or friend.

● Do you seem to struggle more when you're hungry, angry, lonely, or tired? If so, which one seems most difficult for you?

● Try to describe a time when you were stuck in anger.

● How are you coping with family get-togethers these days?

● Is someone in your life pushing you to shape up and move on quickly? If so, how do you respond to this person?

● Write an entry in your journal in which you say things to your parents you want to say, but aren't sure they would receive it in person. After you're done, read it back to God and pray for your parents. If you wish, bring it to a group and read it.

CHAPTER SEVENTEEN

Building Safe Relationships

In the past when friends and neighbors asked, "How are you?" we may have replied, "Fine"—no matter how we felt. Or, "Just great! Couldn't be better!"—when we felt miserable inside. If we had been honest, this is what we would have meant when we said, fine:

F *(fouled up)* **I** *(insecure)* **N** *(neurotic)* **E** *(emotional)*

Some of us have said we're fine when we've felt frustrated or lost because we thought that Christians should always have their little ducks in a row. Donna, the church secretary in the Chapter 2, confesses that she had a double life: her "daytime identity" and her "nighttime identity."

> *At work, I never let people know I was upset. If I had to stay late, I acted cheerful about it. At home, I released my pent-up anger because I knew my husband wouldn't leave me. I yelled at my son and my husband and even threw things at them. The people at church were shocked when I told them about my explosive behavior at home. I see now that my nighttime identity was my outlet. I had to "let down my hair" somewhere because I had felt so unloved in the core of my being. I was trying to please too many people. In the process of crying out for love, I alienated the people I loved most.*

As we grow in our honesty with God, we become more authentic. We try to be the same person all the time — in the workplace, neighborhood, church, and family. This can be difficult if we've been chameleons, changing colors according to where we are and who we're with. This process of learning to say what we really think and feel lets people know us and know what to expect from us so we can build safe relationships.

Living on My Side of The Street

One of the core issues in building safe and honest relationships is for people to have an appropriate sense of how much others have to say in their lives. As children, we may have formed patterns of being too isolated or too needy for attention based on the way we were treated. Now as adults those ruts are so familiar that it's tempting to *continue* in them or *react* to these patterns rather than make wiser choices.

For example, adults who grew up in a home in which

they had little intimacy with parents often *continue* keeping others at a distance. They don't expect to ever bond with anyone socially so they shut people out, resigned that they will never be important to anyone. They may reject love, concern, or wise counsel because they're afraid of feeling abandoned again. In the few relationships they do have, they may not trust easily unless they're in control. They build walls of granite between themselves and others.

Others let too many people have a say in their lives. They can't make a choice until they've asked five people for an opinion because they consider others smarter and wiser. Their boundaries are as permeable as a wall of chicken wire. In childhood, their parents may have made many decisions for them and imposed their wishes on them so that they were entangled and enmeshed with parents.

Sometimes, however, adults don't continue what they learned in childhood, but they *react* to it and seek the opposite. Those raised with walls of granite sense their deep loneliness inside and try to get their needs for attention met from whomever they can, as much as they can. They can't get enough of people. Those who were raised in an enmeshed environment can become tired of consulting people. They want their privacy, and they erect walls of granite around themselves to keep others out.

The task then is to make new balanced boundary

CHILDHOOD PATTERN	CONTINUING THE PATTERN	REACTING TO THE PATTERN
felt distant from parents	remain distant from people	seek too much attention from people
felt entangled with parents	seek too much attention from people	keep distant from people

choices. If that requires skills and insights we don't have, we begin by figuring out the childhood pattern we developed and whether we've continued it or reacted to it. The diagram on page 202 may be helpful.

If you're not sure where you fit, ask yourself these questions:

- Do you open up to few people or to many people?
- Are you more likely to withdraw from people or to wear them out?
- Do you make mistakes and choices because you don't seek anyone's advice or support?
- Do you make mistakes because you don't know how to think for yourself?

If you find that you switch back and forth between being distant and entangled, you're not alone. As we work through boundary issues, we may flip-flop until we find a sense of what's appropriate. To have balanced boundaries means developing a realistic idea of where our concerns begin and end. We don't allow other people to take authority in our concerns and we don't take authority in theirs. My growth is my business, and I'm concerned enough about it that I'll let you attend to your growth. I clean up my side of the street and you clean up yours. I do not trespass on your side of the street in your affairs unless you invite me, and then I do so gently. I alert myself when you trespass on my side of the street and I find polite ways to reestablish my responsibility and authority on my side of the street.

One of the best ways to develop appropriate boundaries is to be around people who respect boundaries. People who respect boundaries don't offer unsolicited advice, but instead ask questions such as, "What about this option? How do you really feel about . . . ?" If they tell us their experiences, they keep in mind that God may be working differently in us than He did in them.

If you have asked too many or too few people for advice in the past, you may be unskilled at choosing who is equipped to give you advice. Ask yourself:

- Do I respect this person?
- Does this person have long-term relationships that show credibility in getting along with others?
- Has this person had similar experiences?
- Does this person seem to look below the surface at motives and feelings?

We need to recognize good counsel and be leery of those who are grandiose enough to think that they know exactly what God wants for us. This is often a subtle cover-up (so subtle they don't realize it) for wanting to control people (because their boundaries aren't appropriate). They may pressure us by saying, "What you need to do is. . . . Everyone knows that. . . ." Sometimes we invite this by our inability to make decisions. If we've grown up with others telling us what to do, we don't make choices easily and we invite meddling. Donna describes how she is learning to respond to people who violate her boundaries.

> *I still feel angry when people ask me a question that is too personal or hint at what I should or shouldn't do. I check myself right away. I rehearse in my mind that my decisions are my own and I'm not obligated to explain them to others. I remind myself that their invasion of my boundaries is inappropriate and it's OK for me to set limits for them. I can choose not to answer their questions, saying perhaps, "I don't think I can talk about that right now."*

If a question is too personal, we have the freedom to say, "I'm not comfortable with that question," or "That's a private matter," or we can change the subject. If someone insists on telling us what we should and shouldn't do, we can reclaim that decision as ours by saying, "I will consider what you've said and pray about it."

As we work to build safe relationships, we need to consider if we violate the boundaries of others. It's easy to do this with the best of intentions. For example, Jane may say to Susie, "I haven't been emotionally honest and God wants me to be more honest about my problems. I think you need to do the same thing." Jane doesn't realize that Susie is learning how to be private. Susie is one of those people who has blurted out her past to everyone she knows. Jane is assuming that what was best for her is best for Susie. She could, perhaps make the suggestion, and then listen to Susie's reply, but to tell her what she needs to do is to violate her boundaries.

The key issue is respect. We respect others, we respect ourselves, and we respect the different ways God works in people. He may heal you in one way and heal me in another. We need to stay away from attitudes that announce:

- I know what's right for your spiritual growth.
- I know what the Bible says you should do.
- I am God's representative to speak to you.

At times, God does speak to us through another person, such as the well-timed advice of Matt's sister, Marcia (chapter 2). If someone offers us advice, we can thank the person and explain that we'll submit it to God for further insight. Then we can wait and see if the advice fits with everything else God is teaching us in our journey. On the other hand, if we believe *we* have meaningful advice for someone else, we can honor that person's boundaries by first sifting our motives before God. If in doubt, it's always better to wait than rush. We must try to do nothing in word or tone that diminishes or talks down to the hearer.

Respect comes from humility. We need to be willing to say:

- I accept that you, like all of us, are human with many limitations.
- I understand that there's probably some pain behind what you're doing.
- I'm not God, and I don't know what you've been through.

Being the Same Person All the Time

Even though examining ourselves draws us into a better relationship with God, it doesn't always help all our relationships. Our open and honest ways of talking about God and our problems can make others feel uncomfortable. Here is an experience Jan has had repeatedly.

It wasn't a good day and it wasn't a bad day. I walked into church and Jennifer said to me, "Hi Jan. How are you?" She waved and smiled.

I gave my usual response, which was true: "Hanging in there."

"That's all?" she said, as she looked at me in shock.

I could see that I had lost a few points on Jennifer's spirituality chart, but it didn't matter to me. Giving up my "looking-good kid" persona at church has freed me to be more genuine with people.

So, I looked at Jennifer, smiled and said, "Yes, that's all." And, *I thought to myself,* God loves me when I'm hanging in there.

If we've set aside the need to be looking-good Christians, we may not fit in so well with people that believe that sunny optimism is a sign of spirituality. Yet these are our brothers and sisters and even though they don't know our struggle, we can be present for them. In our positions as nursery workers, choir members, or Bible teachers, we connect with those who are hurting and allow them to take their masks off without questioning their faith. Being the same person all the time may mean we have to consider the following attitude adjustments.

Abandon your church self

It's our church self that pretends not to be angry and deletes comments from our speech that we think will upset others. Test yourself for a few days and listen to the thoughts you don't dare verbalize to others. *I can't say that. It sounds so un-Christian.* This editing promotes a Jekyll-and-Hyde, church self/real self phoniness.

As an authentic Christian, we listen to angry thoughts and figure out calm, non-threatening ways to ventilate them. We try to avoid saying one thing when we feel the opposite. When someone asks, "How are you?" we don't lie and say we're fine if we're not. We offer the truth, which may be, "I'm growing; sometimes it's not fun," or, "Today, I sense God's strength, but there have been some rough times." The reward for being honest, yet calm is that we find that serenity we've been looking for.

We may also want to experiment with gently challenging others to abandon their church selves by asking, "Tell me—how are you *really* doing?" Some may spill their frustration and even their anger with life. Others may begin to cry.

Understand that every person hurts in some way

The world is full of people who hide hurts behind a careful facade. These "hidden wounded" have emotional scars and may wear masks. We, of all people, can be patient with this kind of denial because we have experienced it. If we are to "clean our side of the street" in this matter, we can pray for those who hurt and ask God to show us if and how He wishes to use us in their lives.

Expect to be distant from some

When we are honest about our hurts and flaws, it may cause some people to avoid us. They may not feel the need or have the ability to talk, trust, or feel as deeply as we do. That does not mean, however, that they are not loved dearly by God. We treat them with respect and we may admire them for many other reasons. They may not be, however, safe people for us to confess to.

We can also try to understand their fear. Each of us (Curt and Jan) wanted to attend church-related support groups for a year but did not do so because we were afraid. *What would Christians think of a Christian therapist who had panic attacks? About a pastor's wife who was mad at God?* Once we became desperate, we finally did attend those groups, but did not reveal our positions to our groups for months until we felt safe.

> *Recognize that no child of God*
> *is more "worthy" than another*

Many of us have served at church hoping to prove ourselves lovable to God. We may even secretly feel that God loves best those who serve more than we do. Here's how Dawn behaved as she came to understand that every person has worth in God's eyes:

> *I used to volunteer for everything. I led children's church even though I wasn't by nature an organizer. I sang in the choir, I baked zucchini bread for continental breakfasts.*
>
> *Once I shed my looking-good kid image, I saw that I was trying to earn God's love. I felt inferior to the other people at church who gave more money than I did, who organized events so well. I felt that God must love them more than He loved me. I realized that my parents treated us kids that way. Whoever did the most was loved the most. For years, I was the Adjuster child and I never stood out like my sister, the Responsible child. As an adult, I tried to fill her role to prove I had finally grown up.*
>
> *Now I see how silly that was. I believe that God loves me as the child He created and that He's bringing me along as fast as I can follow. I'm now interested in a ministry to pregnant teens, and I've found a friend who's a true organizer to help me. I've quit the choir and education committee, which disappointed some people. For once though, I'm following the path I sense God wants me to take rather than saying yes to everything I'm asked to do.*

Develop thick skin

As we learn to take ourselves less seriously, we can set aside other people's remarks or put-downs. Most people have so much to do that they don't have the energy to pick on us intentionally. When they do, they're often responding out of their own hurts and according to their own family roles.

This doesn't mean that we bury hurtful situations. We ventilate them in safe places such as a journal or a confidential small group (leaving the other person nameless). There, we can figure out whether we should confront these situations or disregard them. *Is what this person's doing injuring us or just irritating us? Is confrontation appropriate or helpful?*

Building Community in Marriage

We usually choose whom we'll marry because we like the outward self or "looking-good kid" image of the other person. We may have had only a few glimpses of the other person's real self because sharing ugly thoughts and feelings is not the accepted cultural way to attract a mate. That means many marriages consist of two "looking-good kids," each masking an unpolished, perhaps needy and childish real self. It doesn't take long for those childish real selves to come forth once the safety of marriage is established. Each spouse wants the other's comfort and concern.

In a growing relationship, comfort goes both ways. When only one shares hurts, the relationship becomes stuck. Couples come to marriage counseling and say, "Why did I marry him? Why didn't I see that she was nothing but a taker?" It's important to come to know and accept the needs and worst behaviors of the other person. How does that person behave when he or she is hungry for validation and asking those core questions: *What do I have to do to feel loved? To feel valued?*

Spouses often hope the other will meet needs their

parents didn't meet. Julie knew she was doing this. Her father never held a steady job so she looked for a husband who was ambitious and hard working. Her husband, Mark, hated how his mother had screamed at him daily in childhood, so he found in Julie a quiet, nurturing wife to mother him. Never mind that Julie and Mark had nothing in common with each other. They reacted so strongly against their parents that they didn't marry as wisely as they could have.

Other times we don't know how drastic our needs are until we get into the marriage. Many of us feel desperately needy inside because we fear abandonment. This takes shape in many ways, but this is how it happened to Ann:

When Steve told me that he planned to go to the movies with the guys, I felt left out. But I didn't want to be a nag, so I acted as if nothing were wrong.

But that night when Steve was gone, I remembered the abandonment I felt when my father went drinking. When I was eleven, someone tried to break into our house. My mother and I turned on all the lights in the house and grabbed a baseball bat. We sat in the floor of the hallway next to the phone until the police came. We had no idea where my father was. When he came home, we told him about it and he shrugged his shoulders.

What if someone tried to break in now? I kept wondering. Steve would be gone when I needed him. In my mind, I confronted Steve with times that he had not been there when I needed him. Actually, they weren't that dramatic, but my feelings of abandonment were on a roll and I couldn't stop them. Finally, I went to bed early hoping I would feel better the next day.

But I didn't. I wanted to get back at Steve for "abandoning" me so I invited a co-worker that Steve didn't like to dinner. When she showed up and Steve was annoyed, I looked blank and asked, "Didn't I tell you she was coming?"

Ann knew that her feelings of abandonment were unwarranted, but she couldn't seem to stop feeling them. Her feelings won and she found a way to get back at Steve by inviting her co-worker to dinner. It was too much of a risk to trust Steve, to trust God to take care of Steve, and to trust that she would survive if Steve never came back.

In order for marriages and friendships to work, we need to be willing to hear our own inner cries and admit that a spouse has only a limited role in satisfying those cries. God is the ultimate Satisfier, although He uses people around us at times. We need to work on being able to tell a spouse what we're most afraid of, what we're grasping for in life, what makes us feel loved. That spouse alone cannot meet those needs, but he or she can cooperate with God in getting our needs met as far as he or she is able.

Another dilemma we come across in marriage is that even though we search for a spouse who is not like our King Baby or caretaking parent, we often marry someone like that person anyway. This is reflected by the way that adult children of alcoholics often marry someone who is a substance abuser.[1] Because children are used to chaos and King Babies are used to being taken care of, they subconsciously seek those familiar relationships. The best way to avoid these dilemmas is to begin our journey of self-examination before choosing a spouse.

If you've married without the benefit of self-examination, you can pray for the strength to support each other and hope for both to undergo the examination each of you need. As you become more skilled at listening to yourself, you will probably recognize that you have unknowingly set up roles in marriage that limit your spiritual growth and limit how you can help the other. Here are some common roles that spouses adopt without consciously choosing them.[2]

I'll be the parent, you be the child.
I'll be the smart one, you be the dumb one.

I'll be the worker, you be the player.
I'll be responsible, you can be irresponsible.
I'll be the healthy one, you can be the sick one.
I'll be the leader, you can be the follower.
I'll be the tyrant, you can be the victim.
I'll be decisive, you can be wishy-washy.
I'll be the taker, you can be the giver.
I'll be right, you'll always be wrong.
I'll be the educated one, you can be ignorant.
I'll be friendly, you can be distant.
I'll be the protector, you be the protected.
I'll be hard, you can be soft.
I'll be sensitive, you can be rough.

Part of self-examination involves becoming aware of and then renegotiating these roles on different terms. We may need to admit the role we've played and express a desire to change. We can't change the spouse's behavior, of course, so our change will confuse the relationship. We may have to patiently say, "I'm no longer content to be the designated parent in our relationship, so you will have to take care of this matter yourself," or "I no longer see myself as the dumb one in this relationship, and this is what I think I should do." It behooves us to patient and prayerful if we're the ones that are changing the roles after all these years.

You May Be Wondering . . .

Q *You've implied that many churchgoers are overcoming the problems you've discussed. Why is that?*
A If you limit the discussion to examining the effects of growing up in just alcoholic families, consider this. Focus on the Family received so many requests on the topic of the effects of growing up in an alcoholic family that, in November 1988, they broadcasted their first program about it, repeating it several times. As of that date, they had received more requests from their listeners for this topic than for any

other topic. Among this family-oriented audience with traditional values, these problems from the past were surfacing. Consider then how many more people may react to their childhood of growing up in generally flawed, but non-alcoholic families.

The rate at which Christian support groups are growing is further proof that churchgoers are undergoing this process of self-examination. From the response to that broadcast, the New Hope Support Group at the Evangelical Free Church in Fullerton, California, began compiling a list of support groups and they now number more than 2000. Overcomers Outreach, a network of Christian support groups for people dealing with addictions, includes more than 1000 support groups.

Q *What if I'm seriously dating a person who comes from a family with a raging King Baby parent and a caretaker?*

A It's important to ask the following questions.

1. *Does the person recognize the dynamics of his or her family?* If not, encourage the person to read a book about these things or attend a support group. The person may insist he or she is nothing like his or her King Baby parent or caretaker parent, but the person probably doesn't understand how much havoc the past can create nor its potential for ruining future relationships.

2. *Is the person willing to investigate how his or her background may be affecting him or her right now?* If not, the person may be a victim of his or her pride and a potential trap for you. Being committed to a relationship involves doing whatever work is necessary to learn to express needs and to set boundaries. If the person doesn't understand the needs of his or her real self, he or she will probably expect you to meet his or her needs if you marry. This would be unfair, of course, because no one can meet another person's inner needs.

3. *Are you certain that you didn't seek the person out because you were subconsciously looking for a King Baby or a caretaker?* Even though our conscious mind would disagree, most of us seek to duplicate the tone of our parents' relationship. Examine your motives and needs. Is the relationship characterized by honest communication of feelings or by caretaking, tension, and a violation of boundaries? Would you be dating this person if you felt more secure in God's love and in your self-worth? Ideally, your answers to these questions are yes, but you now have to see if the person will look at his or her childhood issues.

Personal Reflection

Choose three or four of these questions and share the answers with a group or friend.

● Would you say that at your worst moments your boundaries are more likely to be made of granite (distant, not letting anyone in) or chicken wire (entangled, inviting others to have too much of a say in your life)? Mark your place on this continuum.

Granite ———————————————— Chicken wire

● What are you most afraid of in regard to boundaries?

● Do you think your boundaries were entangled, distant, or balanced as a child?

● As an adult, did you:

   continue the same boundary struggle?
   react and choose the opposite style?
   find appropriate boundaries?

● What changes would you need to make to seek more appropriate boundaries?

● Who do you know that is good at giving counsel without telling you what to do?

● Assume for a moment that you have a "church self." What behaviors or phrases would you have to stop doing to abandon that church self, however small it may be? How do you think people will react? Try doing one small thing this week at church to abandon any "church self" behaviors and write down the reactions of people.

● If you have been married or are seriously dating, place a checkmark next to the roles you listed above that you and your spouse have played at times.

● What made one or both of you assume those roles?

● How will it help you to abandon that role? How will it help your spouse?

● How comfortable will you be without that role?

● When would be a good time to discuss these things with your spouse or significant other?

CHAPTER EIGHTEEN

Myths that Sabotage Spiritual Growth

If we want to see God clearly and have an authentic relationship with Him, we may have to work to keep clean the smoked glass windows tainted by our sinful nature, our culture, and our background. We learn to cast off dark and dusty images of God and misconceptions of Scripture that strangle our faith.

We've listed some of these misconceptions below as myths. They seem correct at first because they're based on kernels of truth and then tainted with the idea that denial, blame, and isolation are helpful and that God's anger simmers below the surface, waiting to catch us doing wrong. We have worded them in a blunt way to make them clear, but they come in more subtle versions.

MYTH: Becoming a Christian solves my problems.

TRUTH: Becoming a Christian offers salvation but it doesn't exempt Christians from pain, even pain from the hurts of the past.

Many of us answered the altar call when life wasn't going so well and we were looking for a solution. We may have heard someone say, "Jesus is the answer," so we thought we would "try" him. In this sense, Christianity became a magic potion of sorts to solve problems. This is similar to our culture's magical thinking that the way to solve problems is to buy a new home, marry a new spouse, or move to another state. This "quick fix" approach backfires with faith when people discover that the Christian life is not an easy one. They may become disillusioned and view Christianity as one more thing that didn't work. It can be scary to think, *Not even God can help me.*

The quick fix approach has been known to backfire!

The logical conclusion of this myth is that Christians who do struggle must be lacking in faith. Maybe you've known someone in your church whose been laid off from a job, broad-sided in a car accident, and diagnosed with a chronic disease and wondered, *Why do all those bad things happen to him?* Yet we know that faith doesn't result in a problem-free life because of examples such as: the Old Testament prophet Jeremiah, who sank in the mud of a cistern at the hands of Judah's wicked rulers (Jer. 38:6); Paul, who endured his thorn in the flesh (2 Cor. 12:7-10); Jesus, who suffered to the fullest extent on the Cross. God allows pain and suffering and although He sometimes provides a way out of problems, more often He walks with us through them.

MYTH: Christians have the victory over sin, so sin is only a problem for those with weak faith.

TRUTH: All Christians struggle with sin.

This myth tells people to overcome (actually deny) sin by praising God, claiming the victory, and having an attitude of gratitude. Looking at the past is unnecessary because troubles will cease if you believe hard enough. Those who act within this myth are forced to be overachievers and perfectionists to prove their faith.

Even though God is the divine Physician, He doesn't always heal people or alleviate their struggles with sin. Believers throughout the Bible struggled with sin, including the apostle Paul who described his struggle as a "war" (Rom. 7:23) over which he agonized: "I have the desire to do what is good, but I cannot carry it out. For what I do is not the good I want to do; no, the evil I do not want to do—this I keep on doing. Now if I do what I do not want to do, it is no longer I who do it, but it is sin living in me that does it" (Rom. 7:18-20).

MYTH: Christians should watch out for emotions.

TRUTH: We should experience the feelings God gave us and bring them to Him, especially when we don't understand them.

While we do need to examine our emotions, some people are suspicious of them and speak of disciplining, buffeting or controlling emotions if you want to truly follow God. Curt experienced it this way.

When I was new in my faith, Christians told me, "Curt, don't listen to your emotions. Ignore those feelings and do what God wants you to do." I poured my heart out to one Christian who thumped his Bible and said, "That's just a feeling. What does the Bible say?" He told me that listening to my feelings would get me into trouble. So I ignored my feelings which wasn't difficult—my family had taught me the same thing.

God created feelings. He is a full feeling being, expressing anger (Jonah 4:1), hurt (Hosea 11:1-4), and joy (Neh. 8:10). Much of the Bible talks about feelings, especially in Old Testament poetry and prophecy. King David of the Old Testament, a "man after His [God's] own heart," (1 Sam. 13:14), felt the strength of his emotions and surrendered them to God. We can do the same thing, and struggled with feelings openly:

> *My heart is in anguish within me;*
> *the terrors of death assail me.*
> *Fear and trembling have beset me:*
> *horror has overwhelmed me. . . .*
> *But I call to God,*
> *and the LORD saves me.*
> *Evening, morning and noon*
> *I cry out in distress*
> *and He hears my voice.*
>
> Psalm 55:4-5, 16-17

Cutting off our feelings cuts off a part of who we are. This isolates our emotional lives from our faith and reinforces the chasm between our real self and our church self. How much wiser to deal with feelings, even the ugliest ones, through our faith.

MYTH: Pray and read the Bible more, and you'll grow spiritually.

TRUTH: We come to know God through these two important tools as well as others.

Although prayer and Bible study are two core tools of the Christian, there are other tools that require us to break our isolation. Jesus discipled the apostles by spending time with them, talking with them, asking them questions, and even telling stories. Discipleship is not a solo exercise. In friendships, mentor relationships, and small groups, we hear others' experiences, confess our faults, and experience the love of God. This teaches us to trust God and to trust people.

In worship, we relate to God as the powerful Creator who doesn't abandon us. Worship helps us express back to God the truths of the Scripture in a personal way. We sing and speak directly to God expressing thoughts that may not find their way into our prayers.

MYTH: Christian service means agreeing to do every task the pastor asks me to do.

TRUTH: Burned-out servants give of themselves for wrong reasons, harming themselves and others.

Why is it so difficult to say no to your pastor without feeling a little bit guilty? At some point, Christian service became defined as doing whatever the church needs us to do. We've lost a sense of asking God to show us what it is He has put in our hearts with the gifts He's given us.

The unsettled issues of the past can make us ripe for this kind of derailment of service. Many of us who have been looking-good kids have taken on the work of ministry so that we could hide from our sense of inadequacy. On a deeper level of awareness, we hope that our service will make us feel "good enough," but it doesn't work that way. Self-worth is not based on service, but on God's never failing love for us. If we depend on our performance as a Christian servant to make us feel good about ourselves, even small failures become larger than life. We may even burn out. Jan tells how she discovered this.

> As a pastor's wife, I taught Sunday school, worked in the youth group, sang in the choir, played the piano, and performed any other job I could find to do. I did this partly because I loved God and wanted to serve Him. On another level, I was looking for a way to feel like a success in life, to make up for my sense of inadequacy. As my responsibilities increased and my service failed to produce the results for which I'd hoped, I burned out. I questioned God about why He would allow me to fail.
>
> During my journey of self-examination, I discovered that I was truly a broken person. I saw that I was a King Baby (demanding success from God to prop up my flagging self-worth) and a caretaker (sacrificing myself for everyone else because I

wanted to be loved and noticed). I saw a hidden rage within me that created a drivenness to fix people instead of helping them. I saw that others needed to help instead of relying on me. I realized that I had gone through the motions of serving even when I didn't have time because I unconsciously believed that if I worked for God, He would love me more.

I dropped out of nearly every position and asked God to show me how it was He wanted to use me. As I waited, I felt led to follow some avenues of service I'd never considered before. One was to help others as broken as myself and so I began leading a support group. Instead of being up front, I was tucked away in a back room with people that some in the church referred to as, "the losers." Yet because I was working on letting God fill my needs to be loved and valued, I felt comfortable being hidden in God's back pocket serving in a place where no one would notice me.

When we serve, we need to allow God to speak to us. *Am I doing this to impress anyone? Am I looking for external rewards? Am I using this to feel good about myself? Am I using this to block out God's voice asking me to change my inner self?*

God allows our hearts to be broken by many things around us, and sometimes that breakage becomes a call to do something to help. When that happens, we don't rush in to fix situations. We ask God to show us our role. We're content to wait on Him and let Him direct our path. We look for others who have the same passion and pray for God's leading. When the path is clear and our egos are set aside, we're ready to serve in a way that glorifies God and gratifies the sense of purpose He has put within us.

MYTH: Keep believing and your doubts will fade.

TRUTH: Doubts (or "crises of faith") are a normal part of faith and they can be surrendered to God as we wait for His response.

When we've felt emotionally or physically abandoned in the past, we may find ourselves plagued by doubts about God. We aren't aware of questions that rumble just below the surface until a calamity occurs. *Is God really a Protector? Is Scripture really true? Why is there such a huge gap between what I read in the Bible—"God is love" in 1 John 4:16—and what I feel? Do I really believe what other Christians believe, or have I said this just to please a spouse or a youth director?*

If you bring these doubts up in a Bible study, some may feel uncomfortable because they think that doubts are for unbelievers only. Some may question your faith while others might tell you you're under attack by Satan. While it's true that our spiritual enemy inspires doubts at times, he also inspires the fear that keeps us from addressing them. In the great spiritual warfare passage, Ephesians 6:10-18, the most frequently used word is "stand" (vv. 11, 13-14). If we consider "standing firm" (v. 14) to be our goal in spiritual warfare, we can see the benefit of bringing our doubts before God so He can strengthen our faith-stand in times of darkness.

Many biblical figures "stood firm" against the devil and worked through doubts at the same time. Prophets such as Habakkuk asked God difficult questions as he watched his nation head toward destruction. God didn't reprimand him, but answered those questions. We are standing firm when we explore our doubts in such a way that we don't denigrate God, but admit to our lack of understanding. Working through doubts teaches us to wait on God, to find companionship in Him even when we have no idea of what is going on, to experience the wonder and awe of surrendering to a God who is grand enough to love us in all our humanness. That's why it's wise to find a Christian or two who will listen to us express our crises of faith and help us work through them. Curt tells his experiences processing doubts.

Throughout my Christian life, I professed that God loved me. I believed in my mind that God was there, but I secretly wondered why a loving God hadn't protected me from the chaos of my upbringing. I had a split faith—I claimed a victory in Christ, but I had secret doubts.

Once when I told a pastor about my doubts, he questioned if I truly had a relationship with God. He said I must be harboring some sin in my life. When I told another Christian, she gave me a book on prayer that didn't address my question at all. In the depths of my heart, I began to think there wasn't an answer to my problem.

After that, I kept quiet about my doubts and condemned myself for having them. The more guilty I felt, the less I prayed or served at church. Talking to God only made me feel worse.

Even after I completed my master's degree in psychology and worked as a therapist, I still felt that something was missing. When I began having panic attacks and saw a Christian therapist, I admitted that I doubted God. In the safety of a church-related support group, I admitted that I felt God's promises were empty and they didn't apply to me. Other people admitted the same struggles and we cried together. Some even yelled. I knew I wasn't alone.

After that, I quit condemning myself, which helped me move toward God. Through other people's love and acceptance, I understood God's grace on a deeper level. That opened up a new world of who I was in Christ.

MYTH: Guilt is God's tool to make me good.

TRUTH: Healthy guilt, balanced with unconditional love, spurs our conscience. Shame can cripple us.

Guilt is helpful when it stirs our conscience if we tell a lie or speak harshly to someone. That guilt can motivate us to admit our faults and ask God show us what we need to do to let Him further transform our lives. Guilt doesn't produce this kind of fruit unless we're also convinced we're loved, because love empowers us with hope and tells us that if we confess our sins, God will forgive us (1 John 1:9). Guilt, alone, is hopeless.

When love is missing, we believe we're not only hopeless but also worthless. We lapse into shame, which makes us wonder why we should even try. This doesn't stimulate spiritual growth, but stifles it.

The above myths typify a general attitude of religious shame among some Christians. This shame taints normal events as well as God's good gifts: having fun is bad, having problems is bad, being a sexual person is bad, being ill is bad, being too rich is bad, being too poor is bad. H.L. Mencken described this kind of faith, ". . . the haunting fear that someone, somewhere, may be happy."[1] It promotes unwritten rules such as these:

- Strong people don't cry.
- Spiritual people are always in control.
- Wise people don't ask questions.

The opposites are actually true. People are stronger when they cry; they mature spiritually when they relinquish control to God; wisdom causes us to see fallacies and possible consequences.

If we forget humanity's distorted views of a blaming and shaming God, we see God as a loving Parent full of grace. God does whatever it takes to show us that He loves us, like the woman sifting through the straw floor in the Palestinian hut searching for the lost coin. She lit the lamp, swept the house and searched carefully. She had nine other coins, but she went to great pains to find the tenth. When she found it, she threw a party (Luke 15:8-10). That's the picture of God that we need to understand and remember.

You May Be Wondering . . .

Q *If I'm a "new creation" in Christ (2 Cor. 5:17), doesn't that mean I have overcome sin?*

A Christ purchased our redemption and position in

heaven and we now have the power of the Holy Spirit to equip us (John 14:17; 16:13, 15). Yet this doesn't take away our sin nature and it doesn't cancel the patterns we developed as children and adolescents.

Consider the leaders of the early church, many of whom walked with Jesus and received the Holy Spirit at Pentecost. They struggled with the sin of racial prejudice (probably an influence of their culture) with "much discussion" over Gentiles in the church (Acts 15:7). Everyone on *this side* of heaven struggles with sin.

Q *Why do some people go overboard on expressing feelings when looking at their real selves?*

A Buried feelings have been trapped for years and they can burst open like a breaking dam. One example is the way Matt (Chapter 2) cried uncontrollably when talking to his parents. If we have not expressed feelings very much, we may feel overwhelmed, having never practiced expressing feelings that are so strong. Because it's not easy to express feelings in tactful ways, it may help if when we have something difficult to say, we write down the exact wording and consider our tone of voice. It gives us a chance to consider the impact of our words and rethink what we're going to say. *Will our tears make things worse because this person has been manipulated by tears in the past or perhaps be intimidated by them?*

This isn't to say that we should "live in our feelings," doing whatever they dictate. We listen to our feelings, face whatever truth they may be telling us and discard untruths.

Personal Reflection

Choose three or four of these questions and share the answers with a group or friend.

● Which, if any, of the following myths do you think causes problems for Christians?

Becoming a Christian solves all my problems.

Christians have the victory over sin, so sin is only a problem for the weak in faith.

Christians should watch out for emotions.

Pray and read the Bible more, and you'll grow spiritually.

Christian service means agreeing to do every task the pastor asks me to do.

Keep believing and doubts will fade.

Guilt is God's tool to make me good.

Can you give an example of how these myths have caused problems for you?

● What myths you would like to add to this list?

● What would be most helpful to you in understanding the truth about these myths?

CHAPTER NINETEEN

Wounded Healers as Church Leaders

Before you skip this chapter, consider for a moment your potential as a leader in your church. If you have considered the self-examination presented in this book, you have an authenticity that others will notice. Besides, being a leader means simply that someone else looks up to you. The person you serve with on the finance committee or in the nursery or at a work day may look up to you more than you know. Your children, nieces, nephews, or grandchildren watch you closely, even if you think they don't notice you. As you read this chapter, consider God's role for you in His kingdom.

Building Others Up

As a leader, you can set a tone of vulnerability in these ways.

Catch new Christians before they develop a church self and a real self

What church hasn't wondered about the revolving door that brings people in the front and shuffles them out the back? Why do new Christians back away? Among other reasons, new Christians may not have developed a church self and so they clearly see the discrepancy between who they really are and how they're expected to act. New Christians especially need to examine their distorted views of God, their doubts and motives. They need relationships in which they can be honest about their old behaviors, especially compulsive behaviors. These struggles are rarely addressed in a new members' class.

Don't encourage others to be "looking good kids"

Look through the lens of your heart at those in church who look too good. All that perfection may be hiding deep inner pain that they figure would turn you off if you knew about it. If this is true, they may have hidden it so deeply that they don't even know it's there. Pray for them and share your struggles with them. Perhaps God will use you in their lives.

Form friendships and small groups in which people can examine themselves honestly

Ask God to show you the most open avenues for sharing your vulnerability with others. You might want to meet weekly with a struggling church member or start a support group (see Appendix 1). These efforts will help your church because when people are willing to do the work of self-examination, their relationship with God grows.

Recommend professionals as needed

If your church doesn't have a list of Christian therapists and support groups in the area, you may want to create one. Sadly, the following story has occurred in some churches.

Jessica struggled with bulimia. She attended the church's weekly Bible study and her church friends prayed for her repeatedly. She wanted to go to a therapist, but they told her counseling was a waste of time. She struggled this way for four years, saying to her group, "I would kill myself if I didn't have my sons to raise."

Finally Jessica became so depressed that she lost her job. She applied for government assistance and the social worker insisted she see a psychiatrist at the county clinic. Her church friends told her not to go, but she was so desperate she tried it.

After examining Jessica, the psychiatrist explained that her years of depression had caused a severe chemical imbalance. The psychiatrist wanted to give Jessica medication to balance the chemicals in her body so she could face life with the necessary physiological resources. In the meantime, she went to therapy and a support group to begin recognizing the causes for the depression.

Jessica agreed to take the medication, but decided not to tell her church friends. The depression lifted, and as it did, Jessica examined the reasons behind her bulimia and the issues of her past. Her psychiatrist gradually eased her off the medication and Jessica continued to look at her past and what she needed to do. It took a while, but she got a job and began facing life with more strength than ever before.

To Avoid Misunderstandings
Teach and lead with transparency

Consider the myths in the previous chapter when you prepare a teaching presentation and ask yourself if your lesson reinforces any of the myths. Use examples that deal with common temptations such as sexuality or trying to please and impress others.

If you recruit workers, go out of your way to avoid appealing to caretaking attitudes. Ask, "Is God moving you to do this?" rather than saying, "The church needs you and you're the only one who can do this." Help people operate within their spiritual gifts and the causes that touch their heart.

Acknowledge the struggle of the Christian life

Examine the lessons you teach and your over-the-back-fence counseling to see if they acknowledge that Christians struggle. A good test is to ask how a teen who is being molested by her stepfather would respond to what you plan to say. Ask yourself questions such as these:

- Do I give flip, Christianese answers?
- Do I show empathy for other people's pain?
- Do I balance God's demand for obedience with His love?
- Do I connect people with the resources within our church that can help?
- Do I pray with strugglers afterward rather than simply offering platitudes?

In Mother's Day and Father's Day lessons and devotions, speakers need to admit their struggles as parents and recognize that many adults in the congregation are struggling with memories of parents who abused them. One of the most powerful parts of a lesson or piece of advice is how the person failed and what they did to make amends.

Ask questions more than you give advice. If you think a person is stuck in anger or blame, ask, "What is the next step you need to take?" This shows patience, but also gives direction.

Expect people recovering from compulsions to be blunt and bold communicators

One home fellowship group leader reported that he didn't like it when people from the compulsive behavior support group attended their small group. "They dump all their bad feelings on everybody," he said. "They talk about how they're angry about this and that. They embarrass the rest of us—especially the newcomers."

These situations are ideal times to model honesty and acceptance and to pray for the struggling person. Visitors often follow the leader's behavior. If the leader is embarrassed, the visitor will be too. If the leader is caring yet firm, the visitor will respect the leader's sensitivity and the honesty of the group.

A Special Note to Pastors

Recently, a speaker asked an audience of 800 pastors to raise their hands if their parents or grandparents were alcoholics. Approximately 75% raised their hands. He asked if they had looked at how that might be affecting them, and only a few raised their hands. This makes sense when you consider that both "placaters" and "responsible children" enjoy taking care of people. Being needed makes us feel loved and valued. It can be affirming to hear people say, "You really helped me during my crisis." Compliments on Bible study lessons fill those self-esteem gaps. That's not why people become pastors, of course. You do this because you love God, but without intense self-examination you are unaware of the other factors involved.

Hidden pain

Pastors who are "looking-good kids" have to hide their deeper pain. If they aren't careful, it shows up in caustic comments during the announcements on Sunday or using shame-based techniques to recruit a clean-up crew. At times, the part that imitates the King Baby parent may lord authority over church members; at other times, the caretaker parent side may try to please them all.

Filtered teaching

Even pastors who work at being scholarly or unslanted find that they filter their Bible teaching through their experience. If that experience is full of denial, blame, isolation, and angry responses, the congregation feels the results. When pastors don't understand their distortions about God and cultural myths, they may be slanting the truth for others.

Unhealthy churches

The characteristics listed in Chapters 4 and 5 can also apply to churches. Without realizing it, a pastor can reinforce the same tendencies in a church that existed in the family in which he grew up. You might want to ask your leaders questions such as: "Are the boundaries of individual families overstepped by church leadership? Do people trust each other? Is there consistent reinforcement? Are feelings ever expressed, and if so are they expressed in appropriate ways? Is your church an open or closed system? Are new ideas and independent thinkers welcome?"

Pastors who have worked through a process of self-examination can become "wounded healers" who don't shame people because they're conscious of their own sin. They teach, but they're also learning to listen. Here's an example of a pastor who is now a wounded healer.

Brian had been a pastor for twelve years and was ready to give up. He struggled with pornography daily. After he thought a church member caught him going into an adult book store, he went to see a counselor. He told the counselor that he planned to leave the ministry because he felt he was a complete failure. During the third session, he admitted that he was having an affair.

As Brian and the therapist talked about his past, Brian described his workaholic father. His dad was rarely home and Brian felt emotionally estranged from him. Brian covered his hands with his face and said, "I've preached all this hellfire and damnation because I've been so angry with my father.

*I've counseled people for years and told them that
all their problems came from the sin in their lives. I
used to say, 'If you'll just read the Bible more and
pray, you'll be healed.' I was hardest on people
who struggled with sexual problems because that
was my problem."*

*After a lot of work in counseling and attending
Sexaholics Anonymous groups, Brian faced his addictive behavior. He worked on his marriage and
it was renewed. He began several support groups
in his church and revival has occurred there.*

*At a leadership meeting, Brian told the leaders
about what had happened to him. "I was so afraid
to admit it because I thought they would fire me or
at least laugh at me," says Brian. "They loved me
and accepted me, so I took an even bigger risk. I
told the congregation my story on a Sunday evening. I was terrified, but it went well. It even became a healing service in which hundreds of people admitted their compulsions at the altar. It was
the most exciting thing I've ever seen in the
ministry."*

The results of vulnerable leadership are exciting.
Christians feel free to deal with their crises of faith. They
bear each other's burdens (Gal. 6:2) and encourage each
other to love and do good works (Heb. 10:24).

If God so leads, encourage others to walk through this
valley of vulnerability. Explain that the church would like
to help Christians understand that God is the answer to
the core questions most people are asking — *What must I
do to feel loved and valued?*

Challenge others to look at how they've protected
themselves with masks of refinement. Share your experiences in developing tools of communication and intimacy with others. Our prayer is that you will emerge from
this valley farther down the spiritual path, several steps
closer to God, much more likely to be conformed to His
image.

Personal Reflection

Choose three or four of these questions and share the answers with a group or friend.

● Why do you think wounded healers can be helpful?

● What are some cautions you would offer to wounded healers as leaders?

● In what ways does the local church encourage others to be "looking-good Christians"? How can we avoid that?

● Paul told the Corinthian church: "But He [Jesus] said to me [Paul], 'My grace is sufficient for you, for My power is made perfect in weakness.' Therefore I will boast all the more gladly about my weaknesses, so that Christ's power may rest on me" (2 Cor. 12:9). How does Paul's statement apply to this chapter?

● Compose an ideal prayer for a church leader and pray it to God.

APPENDIX A
What Is A Support Group and How Do I Start One?

If churches are hospitals for sinners instead of hotels for saints, support groups are the intensive care unit. A support group provides a safe setting in which people can talk about feelings and experiences, no matter how ugly they may seem.

To clarify this purpose, let's understand what a support group is not:

- a Bible study, though Scripture may be used;
- group therapy, though there may be interaction;
- a gripe session, though hurts are shared;
- a rehashing of the past, though past events may be related;
- an emotional scene, though some members may cry or get angry.

Watch Out for Fixing

Because Christianity is "the way, the truth, and the life" and Christians know the value of helping others, it's easy to fix each other. If you have listened to many sermons and read many books, it's easy to think you can solve other people's problems. Sometimes, that helpfulness turns into grandiose feelings that we have an answer for nearly every problem. Jan found this to be true.

I had been teaching the Bible for many years when I began attending a support group. In those years, I had done a lot of arm-chair counseling and people always thanked me for helping them so much. I figured I was pretty good at it.

236 / **Healing Hurts that Sabotage the Soul**

*I loved how the support group helped me under-
stand myself, but at first I hated how it didn't allow
me to help others. I found myself thinking that if
that person would just read a certain self-help
book, they would be OK. Every time someone
talked about a problem, I wanted to interrupt and
tell them about a Bible verse that would solve it.
The "no cross talk" rule[1] drove me crazy. I finally
placed my hand over my mouth to remind myself
to keep quiet and listen.*

*I learned some astounding things from this. First,
I learned what a know-it-all, Responsible child/
Placater I am. I honestly thought I could solve the
problems of the people in my group. Then it hit
me — if reading those books could change people,
why hadn't reading them changed me? If I had so
many answers, why was I so broken? I had never
worked through my problems, and that's what I
needed to do. In the support group, I watched others carefully as they worked through problems
week after week until I began doing it myself.*

*As I focused on what others in my support group
were saying instead of planning what I wanted to
say in my sharing time, I was touched by their
lives. Never have so many people influenced me to
change my life with so little intention of doing so.*

Jan would have missed all this if she hadn't obeyed the
standard support group rule of "no fixing." This is the
most difficult problem long-time Christians have in support groups. Here are some tips to try if you're a hard-
core "fixer."

- We remember that our job as a support group
  member is to examine ourselves as honestly as we
  can and to report what we discover about ourselves.
- We don't use our allotted sharing time to offer
  ideas to others, even in subtle ways.
- We affirm others with actions, not words. We hug
  them or pray with them afterward, but we don't

offer either of these in a "quick fix" way. It's tempting to pat them on the hand and say, "You're OK now, aren't you?" No, they're not OK. It will take a while to work through the problem.

- If others ask us for advice after the meeting, we tell them what worked for us, but we don't guarantee it will work for anyone else.

Typical Support Group Format

The following format has been used in small to medium size churches that have one general support group. Use it, adapt it or develop your own materials. If you don't offer child care, exclude #4.

1. The leader introduces himself or herself and welcomes the group.
2. The group repeats the Serenity Prayer:

> *God, grant me the serenity to accept the things I cannot change, the courage to change the things I can, and the wisdom to know the difference.*
> — Reinhold Niebuhr

3. Volunteers from the group read aloud the sections in this Appendix referred to as: *Why a Support Group?, The Problem, The Goal, The Twelve Steps,* and *Tools for Recovery.*
4. The leader passes the hat and explains that a contribution of fifty cents or a dollar helps parents with child care.
5. The leader presents the topic (anger, humility, self-pity, one of the Twelve Steps, or one of the tendencies from Chapter 8 of this book) by sharing a personal example of this from his or her life.
6. The leader reads *Guidelines for Sharing.* Ask: "Who would like to start?" If there is a newcomer or two, the leader may wish to have group members introduce themselves at first, and then say, "Who would like to begin?" The leader closes the sharing (approximately ten minutes before closing).

7. The leader asks group members to share some progress they've made or anything group members would like to be accountable for.

8. The group stands together, holds hands, and closes with a song.

9. Ask that every person greet or hug (if you and they feel comfortable with that) at least two people before leaving.

10. The leader asks group members to help put chairs away.

Why a Support Group?

This group is for:

- those of us who are stuck in some way.
- those of us who can't figure out our kids.
- those of us who feel bogged down in a divorce.
- those of us who are upset with people at work.
- those of us who are trying to overcome habits we hate.

We serve several groups of people:

- those who are stressed out and feeling the strain of seemingly impossible job situations and relationships.
- those in crisis, such as divorce, death, or estrangement from their spouse or children.
- those wishing to resolve past family issues and root through the behaviors that poison their relationships.
- those with compulsive habits, such as overeating, bulimia, overspending, or alcoholism.

In the midst of these problems, we may think thoughts that would shock many people, especially Christians. We may even find ourselves asking the real questions in life:

- Who is God?
- Does He love me?

• If He loves me, how could this happen to me?

Through the acceptance of others in the group, we discover anew that we are truly loved by God, our Heavenly Parent. We can make ourselves accountable to the group, if we wish, to refocus our unhealthy behaviors by surrendering them to God.

A support group is not a class, although information may be shared. It is not a Bible study, although the Bible is the authority on truth. It is not a gripe session, although members may "air dirty laundry." It is not a therapy group, although we do work through experiences. It is not a healing session, although we do ask God to give us the hope we need so badly.

The Problem

Whether we are crushed in crises or haunted by unhealthy habits, we may find ourselves doing and saying things we never thought ourselves capable of. Feelings of anger, disappointment, and fear come up and we're not sure how to resolve them.

Even though we would like to gripe, blame, and find fault with others, we do not. Instead, we choose to look within and admit our unhealthy habits, unhealthy patterns of relating to others, and even our disappointment with God.

We have stuffed many of our feelings and sometimes we have difficulty feeling or expressing our negative emotions because they hurt so much. Our comfortable feelings such as joy or happiness can be difficult to express too. We slip into living life based on these three unwritten rules: Don't talk, don't trust, don't feel.

We sometimes identify with one or more of these tendencies:

Distrust

• overreacting to uncontrollable circumstances

- lying when it would be just as easy to tell the truth
- making decisions based on whim or intense analysis

Self-Condemnation

- judging self without mercy
- seeking approval and affirmation
- being loyal to people that hurt us

Alienation

- fearing abandonment
- struggling with intimate relationships
- feeling less adequate than others

Tension

- working at having fun
- taking self too seriously
- acting irresponsibly or super-responsibly
- creating chaos wherever we go

The Goal

We're learning to look to God, our Heavenly Father, as the initiator of our new lives. He can direct us toward a life of wholeness and healing of the past. We learn that we do not have to be ruled by crises or imprisoned by our pasts.

Here are some goals we may choose:

- To surrender our hurts and patterns of denial, blame, isolation, and anger to God, knowing that only He can turn our lives in a new direction.
- To examine how our present behaviors may be rooted in our lack of understanding that God loves us and values us.

- To forgive parents and release them to God.
- To detach from whatever or whomever we may be obsessed with: our needs, our spouses, our children, our parents, our friends.
- To love ourselves and others, even though this may take the form of "tough love."
- To learn that real love cannot exist without the dimension of justice—in other words, we can love someone and still ask that they respect us.
- To acknowledge our feelings and express them in healthy ways.
- To surrender to God our false guilt and be freed from the shame that has bound us.
- To quit seeing ourselves as someone who can "fix" and take care of others—that's God's job only.

Format for the New Hope Support Group

The New Hope support group at the Evangelical Free Church in Fullerton, California, has a well-developed support group program, one of which is geared to Adult Children of Dysfunctional Families (ACDF), which includes all of us to some degree. This group developed the following format, which you are welcome to use or adapt if you wish.

New Hope meets in the morning and in the evenings. The meetings last an hour and a half.

Part 1—Opening (25 minutes)

1. The leader for that evening introduces himself or herself and welcomes the group.
2. The group repeats the Serenity Prayer:

God, grant me the serenity to accept the things I cannot change, the courage to change the things I can, and the wisdom to know the difference.

Living one day at a time, enjoying one moment at a time, accepting hardship as a pathway to peace;

taking, as Jesus did this sinful world as it is, not as I would have it, trusting that You will make all things right if I surrender to Your will; so that I may be reasonably happy in this life and supremely happy with You forever in the next. Amen.

— Reinhold Niebuhr

3. Volunteers from the group read material similar to *The Problem* and *The Goal* (see pages 239–241), mostly from New Hope pamphlet.

4. The leader gives announcements and a short testimony. The meeting is dismissed allowing five minutes to move to small groups.

Part 2 — Small Groups (60 minutes)

The leaders of small groups read the following rules for small group discussion.

Rules for Small Group Discussion

1. While others are talking, please let them finish without interruption.

2. No fixing — we are to listen, to support, and to be supported by each other in the group, not to give advice. Please save any questions until after the group is dismissed.

3. Speak in the "I" form instead of "we," "they," or "you." This helps us take responsibility for our feelings and accept them as being valid. Examples: "I believe . . ." rather than, "They say . . ." "I felt angry that . . ." rather than, "She made me so angry."

4. Keep sharing to no more than five minutes in order for others in the group to be able to share.

5. Try to share from the heart as honestly as you can. It's OK to cry, laugh, be angry in the group without condemnation from others.

6. What is shared and who you see in the group is to stay in the group and not to be shared with anyone else.

Participants choose from the following groups to attend. Completing the Newcomers program is a prerequisite to attending the other groups. The leaders of New-comers groups read the following rules.

Newcomers (6 weeks)

Weeks 1–3: Visitors are introduced to the problems of Adult Children of Dysfunctional Families (ACDF) through a three-part video that New Hope has produced. It features group members who share their experiences and Pastor Dave Carder who explains how God is in the process all the way. Each week includes one segment of the video and then participants divide into groups of ten and share their reactions or ask questions.

Weeks 4–6: Facilitators spend one week each presenting the four ACDF roles, the three unwritten rules (Don't talk, don't trust, don't feel), and the characteristics of birth order. Once again, participants divide into groups of ten and share their reactions or questions. (Material for weeks 4–6 may be found in Chapter 8 of this book and books such as *The Birth Order Book* by Kevin Leman, Revell, 1985.)

15 Characteristics (open groups—ongoing)

These groups of about ten people discuss the characteristics of Adult Children of Alcoholic/Dysfunctional Families using Christian Twelve Step guidelines such as *The Twelve Steps—A Spiritual Journey* (Recovery Publications, pp. 1-4). It is an "open" group in that anyone who has attended Newcomers may attend it, and it does not require a commitment of consistent attendance.

13 Characteristics (closed groups—13 weeks)

These closed discussion groups are limited to an agreed-upon number of people who decide to commit themselves to working together for a specific period of time. These groups discuss one of the 13 characteristics as found in Janet G. Woititz' *Adult Children of Alcoholics*

(Health Communications, Inc., 1983, p. 4) each week. These are similar to the list in Chapter 8 of this book.

12-Step Study (closed groups—16 weeks)

These discussion groups, which are often assigned, use *The Twelve Steps—A Spiritual Journey* (Recovery Publications, pp. 5–147). This takes sixteen weeks instead of twelve weeks because some of the steps, especially Step four, require more than one week. This group also has a twenty-eight week format for a slower study of the steps.

Managing New Hope
Facilitator Training

These eight-week sessions are held before the regular meetings. Those volunteers who wish to lead small groups must presently participate in New Hope and must have participated for at least twenty weeks. They are trained to handle support group situations, not to act as therapists or teachers. They are "fellow travelers" who continue to work on their own recovery and helps their groups remain a safe place.

New Hope Council

The New Hope Council consists of five volunteers who divide up the responsibilities of ordering materials, organizing set up and clean up, organizing refreshments, assigning testimonies and greeters, handling money, and managing the book table. The members serve for thirteen weeks. They were originally chosen by the ministry leader, but now they find their own replacements and terms are staggered.

Resources

New Hope currently offers resources such as the New Hope Video, a facilitator training manual, characteristic study guides, and an international list of Christian adult children of dysfunctional families support groups. Send requests for products or a price list to this address:

New Hope Support Group
First Evangelical Free Church
2801 North Brea Blvd.
Fullerton, CA 92635-2799
714/529-5544

APPENDIX B
Support Group Resources

If you would like to start a support group in your church, consider contacting the organizations listed below. Some offer printed materials while others offer workshops and conferences. For more information about groups, contact the Self-Help Clearinghouse: 201/625-7101 (TTD: 201/625-9053).

Christian Networks and Centers

Alcoholics for Christ
Michael O' Keefe, Program Coordinator
1316 North Campbell Road
Royal Oaks, MI 48067
800/441-7877
Network of groups (including Adult Children of Alcoholics), printed materials, leadership training

Confident Kids
Linda Kondracki, Executive Director
721 W. Whittier Blvd., Suite H
La Habra, CA 90631
310/697-6201
Network of groups, printed materials, leadership training

ELEEO Ministries, Inc.
Bill and Pat Elam
1229 Rita Ave.
St. Charles, IL 60174
708/584-0460
Network of groups, conferences, facilitator training, printed materials

Free to Care Ministries
P. O. Box 1491
Placentia, CA 92670-9491
714/528-5413
Clearinghouse for counselors, workshops, videos, leadership training for survivors of sexual abuse groups

ICL Renewed Life Services
Vernon Bittner, Executive Director
P. O. Box 47482
Plymouth, MN 55447
612/593-1791
Network of groups, printed materials, leadership training

National Association for Christian Recovery
P. O. Box 11095
Whittier, CA 90603
310/697-6201
Conference, magazine, workshops, clergy network, mental health professional network, resource directory

Overcomers of Brevard, Incorporated
Ron Ross, Executive Director
4235 Mt. Sterling Ave.
Titusville, FL 32780
407/264-0757
Network of groups, leadership training

Overcomers Outreach, Inc.
Judy Turnbull, Director
2290 West Whittier Blvd.
La Habra, CA 90631
310/697-3994
Nationwide network of groups, printed materials

Rapha, Inc.
12700 North Featherwood #250
Houston, TX 77034
800/383-4673
Network of groups, printed materials, leadership training

Rancho Capistrano
Beth Funk, Director
28251 Camino Capistrano
San Juan Capistrano, CA 92675
714/347-7864
Weeks of restoration and renewal with support groups and speakers

Recovery Works!
Stephen Smith
P. O. Box 226
Washougal, WA 98671
206/835-2738
Video & printed resources for support group leadership training, speaking engagements, personal growth coaching

Safekey Ministries
Kim Ensworth, Director
P. O. Box 92762
Henderson, NV 89009
800/NEW-HUGS
Network of groups, workshops, printed materials, audio tapes, leadership training

Twelfth Step Outreach
1201 Knoxville Street
San Diego, CA 92110-3718
619/275-6639
Workshops, printed materials, leadership training

Secular Groups

Adult Children of Alcoholics
Central Service Board
P. O. Box 3216
Torrance, CA 90505
310/534-1815
Network of groups, printed materials

Al-Anon/Alateen
Family Group Headquarters, Inc.
P. O. Box 862 Midtown Station
New York, NY 10018
212/302-7240
Network of groups, printed materials

Alcoholics Anonymous
World Services, Inc.
475 Riverside Drive
New York, NY 10115
212/870-3400
Network of groups, printed materials

Children of Alcoholics Foundation
P.O. Box 4185
Grand Central Station
New York, NY 10163
212/754-0656
Printed information, videos

Co-Dependents Anonymous (CODA)
P.O. Box 33577
Phoenix, AZ 85067-3577
602/277-7991
Network of groups, printed information

Emotions Anonymous
P.O. Box 4245
St. Paul, MN 55104
612/647-9712
Network of groups, printed information

National Association for Children of Alcoholics
P.O. Box 3216
Torrance, CA 90510
310/534-1815
Network of groups, printed information

Narcotics Anonymous World Service Office
16155 Wyandotte Street
Van Nuys, CA 91406
818/780-3951
Network of groups, printed information

Overeaters Anonmyous
P.O. Box 92870
Los Angeles, CA 90009
213/542-8363
Network of groups, printed information

Workaholics Anonymous
P.O. Box 289
Menlo Park, CA 94026-0289
510/859-5804
Network of groups, printed information

A P P E N D I X C
What Is Recovery and How Does It Help?

The attitudes and approaches of Twelve Step groups such as Alcoholics Anonymous have come to be called "recovery." Much of the AA philosophy is rooted in Scripture because Bill Wilson, the co-founder of AA, relied on religious sources, some of whom were Christian.

Over the years, the AA model has become the most successful method for treating alcoholism and, says Newsweek, "There are . . . few, if any, alcohol treatment centers in the United States that do not funnel their outpatients into AA."[1] People with other compulsions have found that the AA methods work for them too, and so now there are many Twelve Step groups including Overeaters Anonymous, Debtors Anonymous, Emotional Health Anonymous, and others. Groups called Adult Children of Alcoholics (ACA) groups began following this pattern as well. Some have found that the ACA tendencies fit them well, but they didn't grow up in alcoholic families. They have been informally called "Adult Children of Dysfunctional Families" and often attend Co-Dependents Anonymous meetings. (See Appendix B.)

We believe Twelve Step groups succeed because they provide places of safety through their acceptance and rigorous honesty.

What Does Recovery Have to Offer Christians?

Some Christians are suspicious of recovery, thinking that it's unrelated to faith and obedience, while others have used the Christian-based principles in AA to face roadblocks in their relationship with God. Some of the Chris-

251

tian distinctives of recovery are these (biblical references not included here follow after the Twelve Steps below):

Our parents' sins affect us

Unlike humanists, Christians believe that all have sinned (Rom. 3:23). When parents sin, it affects their children (Deut. 5:9-10). As Christians grow spiritually, they may also continue to mimic the fallen tendencies they saw in their parents as they were growing up. Recovery groups provide a safe place to express hurt and anger and begin to let go of these tendencies.

Regular self-examination

Taking a fearless moral inventory, listing persons we have harmed and making amends (repeated concepts in the Twelve Steps) get to the heart of protective behavior and pain-management addictions. The warmth and acceptance of a support group helps members look at their defects of character (lack of love, joy, peace, and so on) with God's grace.

Confessing sins and becoming accountable to others facilitates healing

The recovery distinctives of admitting defects of character to a mentor/sponsor or a group who is pledged to confidentiality are important faith elements and follow the Christian concept of discipleship.

Thinking right thoughts isn't enough

If thinking right thoughts could change people, God would have been satisfied with giving the Ten Commandments to Moses. More was needed for the world to have a relationship with His Son who can provide love, forgiveness, and direction. God provided truth in the form of this relationship because people change as they interact with others, not in isolation. The church functions as a family in which we absorb truth. The Twelve Step movement acknowledges that people need each other and they need to work through truths by talking about them.

Spiritual disciplines provide a path to knowing God

The Twelve Steps speak of meditation and conscious contact with God (practicing the presence of God) — distinctive spiritual disciplines. Attendees are encouraged to use tools that have long been honored in Christian traditions: confession, accountability, meeting together regularly, discipleship (sponsoring), journaling, prayer, restitution (making amends), reading Scripture, and other appropriate literature.

A Short History of Recovery
Non-Experts Excel in an Era of Experts

Throughout history people have gathered to listen, to talk, and to solve problems together. Hunters swapped stories over campfires; mothers shared insights as they washed their clothes in the river. As knowledge has become more specialized, it's been assumed that only experts in certain fields can help people. Before Alcoholics Anonymous was created in 1935, experts proposed various solutions for alcoholism, but nothing worked.

- Medical experts medicated alcoholism with drugs to stop the physical act of drinking.
- Psychologists helped alcoholics resolve problems so they would no longer need to drink. This didn't "cure" alcoholics because they had formed life-long habits of using alcohol to manage pain.
- Religious experts (pastors) urged alcoholics to call on God to miraculously stop the craving for alcohol. Some were healed, but many weren't.[2]

This left people like Bill Wilson, a New York stockbroker, and Dr. Bob Smith, an Akron physician, feeling hopeless. Finally Bill stopped drinking through a spiritual experience he had after meeting with a medical doctor friend. Yet when Bill went to Akron on business, he felt the need to drink so he used the method he had used in New York — talking with another alcoholic. That alcoholic was Dr. Bob, who then became sober too and they began visiting alcoholics at a local hospital. These recovering alcoholics started a group in Akron and then in New York.[3]

Bill Wilson and the early groups developed the Twelve Steps as a spiritual path to recovery (see below). One reason the Twelve Step progression worked was that it combined all three approaches: *Physical* — alcoholics became accountable to the group to avoid drinking just one day at a time; *Psychological* — alcoholics dealt with defects of character and underlying issues, and AA, as a support group, reinforced those who stayed sober and accepted practicing alcoholics as long as they wished to get better; *Spiritual* — alcoholics quit trying to control themselves and instead surrendered to a Higher Power; they recognized that their drinking was a result of their defects of character and began identifying those defects and making amends.

These pioneering "non-experts" used various tools such as anonymity and confidentiality (mentioned in the Twelve Traditions) to insure the safety necessary for alcoholics to be honest.

The Twelve Steps and The Twelve Traditions

When members of Twelve Step groups talk about "working a program," they refer to putting the Twelve Steps of AA into action. Listed below are the Twelve Steps of Alcoholics Anonymous, reworded for the Adult Child of the Dysfunctional Family by the New Hope group.

Step 1 We admitted we were powerless over our separation from God — that our lives had become unmanageable. (The original AA wording says, "powerless over alcohol.")

Scripture: "I know that nothing good lives in me, that is, in my sinful nature. For I have the desire to do what is good, but I cannot carry it out" (Romans 7:18).

The idea of powerlessness is difficult for people because they believe that they are in charge of themselves and their environment. Our culture's rugged individualism and success ethic says that anyone who tries hard enough can overcome. This first step asks participants to be humble enough to recognize that there are forces greater than themselves.

Step 2 We came to believe that a power greater than ourselves could restore us to sanity. Scripture: "For it is God who works in you to will and to act according to His good purpose" (Philippians 2:13).

This step acknowledges that man alone cannot help himself, but needs to rely on a greater power.

Step 3 We made a decision to turn our will and our lives over to the care of God as we understood Him. Scripture: "Therefore, I urge you, brothers, in view of God's mercy, to offer your bodies as living sacrifices, holy and pleasing to God—this is your spiritual act of worship" (Romans 12:1).

This step describes surrender to God. These first three steps are often abbreviated: (1) I can't, (2) God can, (3) I'll let Him.

Step 4 We made a searching and fearless moral inventory of ourselves.

Scripture: "Let us examine our ways and test them, and let us return to the LORD" (Lamentations 3:40).

In a Twelve Step inventory, participants comb through their lives looking for character defects in themselves, but not in others.

Step 5 We admitted to God, to ourselves, and to another human being the exact nature of our wrongs.

Scripture: "Therefore, confess your sins to each other and pray for each other so that you may be healed" (James 5:16a).

Confession to God and others helps participants know and say the truth about themselves.

Step 6 We were entirely ready to have God remove all these defects of character.

Scripture: "Humble yourselves before the Lord, and He will lift you up" (James 4:10).

Once participants recognize character defects (Step 5), they go on to become willing to change (Step 6).

Step 7 We humbly asked Him to remove our shortcomings.

Scripture: "If we confess our sins, He is faithful and just and will forgive us our sins and purify us from all unrighteousness" (1 John 1:9).

Participants find their willingness to change strong enough that they ask God to change them.

Step 8 We made a list of all persons we had harmed and became willing to make amends to them all.

Scripture: "Do to others as you would have them do to you" (Luke 6:31).

Participants take personal responsibility for actions, own up to mistakes, and find ways to make restitution.

Step 9 We made direct amends to such people wherever possible, except when to do so would injure them or others.

Scripture: "Therefore, if you are offering your gift at the altar and there remember that your brother has something against you, leave your gift there in front of the altar. First go and be reconciled to your brother; then come and offer your gift" (Matthew 5:23-24).

Step 10 We continued to take personal inventory and when we were wrong promptly admitted it.

Scripture: "So, if you think you are standing firm, be careful that you don't fall!" (1 Corinthians 10:12)

Self-examination is a life-long process.

Step 11 We sought through prayer and meditation to improve our conscious contact with God as we understood Him, praying only for knowledge of His will for us and the power to carry that out.

Scripture: "Let the word of Christ dwell in you richly" (Colossians 3:16a).

Changing behavior requires personal contact with God.

Step 12   Having had a spiritual awakening as a result of these steps, we tried to carry this message to others, and to practice these principles in all our affairs.

Scripture: "Brothers, if someone is caught in a sin, you who are spiritual should restore him gently. But watch yourself, or you also may be tempted" (Galatians 6:1).

The Twelve Traditions

Some of the Twelve Traditions that AA and other Twelve Step groups use transfer directly to a church-related support group. Others do not, because many churches require one designated leader who is accountable to the church. These traditions reveal the spirit in which AA was developed and show how it has avoided becoming entangled in any purpose other than recovery from alcoholism.

One — Our common welfare should come first: personal recovery depends upon AA unity.

Two — For our group purpose there is but one ultimate authority — a loving God as He may express Himself in our group conscience. Our leaders are but trusted servants; they do not govern.

Three — The only requirement for AA membership is a desire to stop drinking.

Four — Each group should be autonomous except in matters affecting other groups or AA as a whole.

Five — Each group has but one primary purpose — to carry its message to the alcoholic who still suffers.

Six — An AA group ought never to endorse, finance, or lend the AA name to any related facility or outside enterprise, lest problems of money, property and prestige divert us from our primary purpose.

Seven — Every AA group ought to be fully self-supporting, declining outside contributions.

Eight — Alcoholics Anonymous should remain forever nonprofessional, but our service centers may employ special workers.

Nine — AA, as such, ought never be organized; but we may create service boards or committees directly responsible to those they serve.

Ten — Alcoholics Anonymous has no opinion on outside issues; hence the AA name ought never be drawn into public controversy.

Eleven — Our public relations policy is based on attraction rather than promotion; we need always maintain personal anonymity at the level of press, radio, and films.

Twelve — Anonymity is the spiritual foundation of all our Tradition, ever reminding us to place principles before personalities.[4]

Because church-related support groups do not follow all of these Twelve Traditions, they are not Twelve Steps groups in the purest sense of the AA tradition. True Twelve Step groups have no leaders. The groups may meet in a church building, but they are never affiliated with any church.

You May Be Wondering . . .

Q Is Alcoholics Anonymous a Christian organization?

A Alcoholics Anonymous is not a distinctly Christian organization. The phrase, "Higher Power," originally referred to God[5], but this inclusive language drew agnostics[6] as well. Eventually Jews, Hindus, Moslems, and Buddhists joined the fellowship,[7] which made the writers of *Alcoholics Anonymous* (also called the Big Book) glad because they wanted alcoholics of all faiths to recover. The Big Book is sprinkled with the words, "God," "faith" and "spiritual," but faith in Christ is not mentioned. AA is spiritual in that it reminds alcoholics to allow their spiritual natures to participate in alcohol recovery, but the purpose of the group is to help them find sobriety, not a specific faith.

Various Christian traditions have reacted differently

to AA. When the Big Book was published, clergyman Dr. Harry Emerson Fosdick reviewed it with approval.[8] Today some churches favor Twelve Step groups so much that they go out of their way to have Twelve Step meetings held at their facilities. On the other hand, some Christians have dismissed Twelve Step meetings as "New Age" and maintain that the Higher Power is Satan. In recent years, atheists have objected to AA, saying that sobriety and spirituality have nothing to do with each other. They have formed their own network, Secular Organizations for Sobriety (SOS).

Q *Can I talk about my faith at regular Twelve Step meetings?*

A While most Twelve Step meetings are secular, meaning that they have no religious connections, it's not unusual for someone at a meeting to name their Higher Power as Jesus Christ. Some who attend these groups have said they don't like it when Christians "act like AA is church." (Technically, this is crosstalk, but it's defended as merely sharing of feelings.) Different meetings vary greatly in tone. Christians can and do find support from secular Twelve Step meetings.

The Twelve Steps

1. We admitted we were powerless over alcohol—that our lives had become unmanageable.

2. Came to believe that power greater than ourselves could restore us to sanity.

3. Made a decision to turn our will and our lives over to the care of God as we understood Him.

4. Made a searching and fearless moral inventory of ourselves.

5. Admitted to God, to ourselves, and to another human being the exact nature of our wrongs.

6. Were entirely ready to have God remove all these defects of character.

7. Humbly asked Him to remove our shortcomings.

8. Made a list of all persons we had harmed and became willing to make amends to them all.

9. Made direct amends to such people wherever possible, except when to do so would injure them or others.

10. Continued to take personal inventory and when we were wrong promptly admitted it.

11. Sought through prayer and meditation to improve our conscious contact with God, as we understood Him, praying only for knowledge of His will for us and power to carry that out.

12. Having had a spiritual awakening as a result of these steps, we tried to carry this message to others, and to practice these principles in all our affairs.

NOTES

Chapter 3. Questions at the Crossroads
1. This is an informal observation of physician Dr. Willard Hawkins from his private medical practice with Harbor Family Practice in Fullerton, California.

2. Daniel J. Levinson with Charlotte N. Darrow, Edward B. Klein, Maria H. Levinson, and Braxton McKee, *The Seasons of a Man's Life* (New York: Ballantine Books, 1978), 57–62.

Chapter 4. The Handicap of Being Human
1. "Don't talk, don't trust, don't feel" are three rules that Claudia Black popularized in her book, *It Will Never Happen to Me* (Denver, CO: M.A.C. Printing and Publications Division, 1982), Chapter 3, 31–52.

2. David Seamands, *Healing for Damaged Emotions* (Wheaton, IL: Victor Books, 1989), 69.

Chapter 5. Patterns that Block Our Growth
1. "National Association for Children of Alcoholics," National Association for Children of Alcoholics (South Laguna, CA: NACoA).

2. "Children of Alcoholics Battle Trauma as Adults," *Los Angeles Times,* 24 September 1985, sec. V.

3. "Gene Associated with Alcoholism Identified," *UCLA News,* 17 April 1990.

4. "National Association for Children of Alcoholics," National Association for Children of Alcoholics (South Laguna, CA: NACoA).

Chapter 6. The Way Families Tend to Be
1. From an interview with Jan Frank, author of *Door of Hope* and *When Victims Marry.*

2. M.L. Kammeier, "Adolescents From Families With and Without Alcohol Problems," *Quarterly Journal of Studies on Alcohol* 32, (1971): 364–72.

3. I. Nylander, "Children Of Alcoholic Fathers," *Acta Paediatrica* 49, no. 1 (1960): 1–134.

4. J.R. Morrison and M.A. Steward, "A Family Study of the Hyperactive Syndrome," *Biological Psychiatry* 3 (1971): 189–95, and D.P. Cantwell, "Psychiatric Illness in the Families of Hyperactive Children," *Archives of General Psychiatry* 27 (1972): 414–17.

5. E.W. Fine, L.W. Yudin, J.Holmes, and S. Heinemann, "Behavioral Disorders in Children With Parental Alcoholism," *Annals of the New York Academy of Sciences* 23 (1976): 507–17.

261

6. J.F. McLachlan, R.L. Walderman, and S. Thoman, "A Study of Teenagers With Alcoholic Parents," *Donwood Institute Research Monograph* 3 (1973); P.A. O'Gorman, "Self-Concept, Locus on Control, and Perception of Father in Adolescents From Homes With and Without Severe Drinking Problems" (Ph.D. diss., Fordham University, 1975); J. Hughes, "Adolescent Children of Alcoholic Parents and the Relationship of Alateen to These Children," *Journal of Consulting and Clinical Psychology* 45, no. 5 (1977): 946–47; and D.W. Goodwin, F. Schulsinger, L. Hermansen, S.B. Guze, "Psychopathology in Adopted and Nonadopted Daughters of Alcoholics," *Archives of General Psychiatry* 34 (1977): 1005–9.

7. J. Hughes, "Adolescent Children of Alcoholic Parents and the Relationship of Alateen to These Children," *Journal of Consulting and Clinical Psychology* 45, no. 5 (1977): 946–47; D. Miller and M. Jang, "Children of Alcoholics: A Twenty-Year Longitudinal Study," *Social Work Research and Abstracts* 13 (1977): 23–29; M.E. Chafetz, H.T. Blane, and M.J. Hill, "Children of Alcoholics: Observations in a Child Guidance Clinic," *Quarterly Journal of Studies on Alcohol* 31 (1971): 687–98.

8. "Why Stress Makes You Stupid," *M Magazine* (May 1988): 72.

9. Erik Erikson, *Childhood and Society* (New York: W.W. Norton, 1963), 247–73.

Chapter 7. Roles that Get Us Through Childhood

1. These roles were noted and named by Claudia Black in her book *It Will Never Happen to Me* (MAC Publishing, 1982). Sharon Wegscheider-Cruse in *Another Chance: Hope and Health for the Alcoholic Family* (Science and Behavior Books, Inc., 1989) uses other names for similar roles, which we have also included.

Chapter 8. Scrambling to Be Adults

1. Janet Geringer Woititz originated these specific characteristics in her book *Struggle for Intimacy,* (Pompano Beach, FL: Health Communications, 1985), 85–98. We have placed them in a different order and provided our own comments.

Chapter 9. Numbing the Pain

1. For more information about this problem, see *When Food Is Your Best Friend* and *Surrendering Hunger* by Jan Johnson (HarperSanFrancisco, 1993).

2. D.W. Goodwin, F. Schulsinger, L. Hermansen, S.B. Guze, and G. Winokur, *Archives of General Psychiatry* 28 (1973): 238–43.

3. Patrick Carnes, *Out of the Shadows* (Minneapolis, MN: CompCare Publications, 1983): 26–47.

Chapter 10. Blurred Spiritual Vision

1. David Seamands, *Healing of Memories* (Wheaton, IL: Victor Books, 1985), 98–99.

2. Lawrence O. Richards, *The Teacher's Commentary* (Wheaton, IL: Victor Books, 1988), 729.

Chapter 11. The Examined Life

1. Popularly attributed to Reinhold Niebuhr.

Chapter 12. Listening to Ourselves
1. Hugh Missildine, M.D., *Your Inner Child of the Past* (New York, NY: Simon & Schuster, 1963), 1–50.

Chapter 14. Admitting who We Are
1. Karl Menninger, *Whatever Became of Sin?* (New York: Hawthorne, 1972), 25.

Chapter 15. Tools for Creating Safe Places
1. Samuel A. Schreiner, Jr., "Why Do We Cry?" *Reader's Digest*, February 1987, 141.
2. James Pennebaker, *Opening Up The Healing Power of Confiding in Others* (New York, NY: Avon Books, 1990), 50.

Chapter 17. Building Safe Relationships
1. Deborah Helen Krois, "Children of Alcoholics" (Ph.D. diss., Biola University, 1987), 32.
2. Roger L. Gould, M.D., *Formations Growth and Change in Adult Life* (New York: Simon & Schuster, 1978), 279.

Chapter 18. Myths that Sabotage Spiritual Growth
1. Jon Winokur, ed., *The Portable Curmudgeon* (New York: New American Library, 1987), back cover.

Chapter 19. Wounded Healers as Church Leaders
1. Jon Winokur, ed., *The Portable Curmudgeon* (New York: New American Library, 1987), back cover.

Appendix A   What Is A Support Group and How Do I Start One?
1. The "no crosstalk" rule means that participants may not interrupt each other, correct each other, or advise each other.

Appendix C   What Is Recovery and How Can It Help?
1. Charles Leershen et al., "Unite and Conquer," *Newsweek*, 5 February 1990, 55.
2. We are indebted to psychologist Dr. Earl Henslin for his study of the AA movement and for these observations.
3. Facts taken from "Foreword to Second Edition," *Alcoholics Anonymous* (New York: Alcoholics Anonymous World Services, 1976), xv-xxi.
4. *Alcoholics Anonymous,* (New York: Alcoholics Anonymous World Services, 1976), 564.
5. "We Agnostics" in *Alcoholics Anonymous* (New York: Alcoholics Anonymous World Services, 1976), 45.
6. "We Agnostics" in *Alcoholics Anonymous* (New York: Alcoholics Anonymous World Services, 1976), 44.
7. "Foreword to Second Edition" in *Alcoholics Anonymous* (New York: Alcoholics Anonymous World Services, 1976), xx.
8. "Foreword to Second Edition," in *Alcoholics Anonymous* (New York: Alcoholics Anonymous World Services, 1976), xvii-xviii.